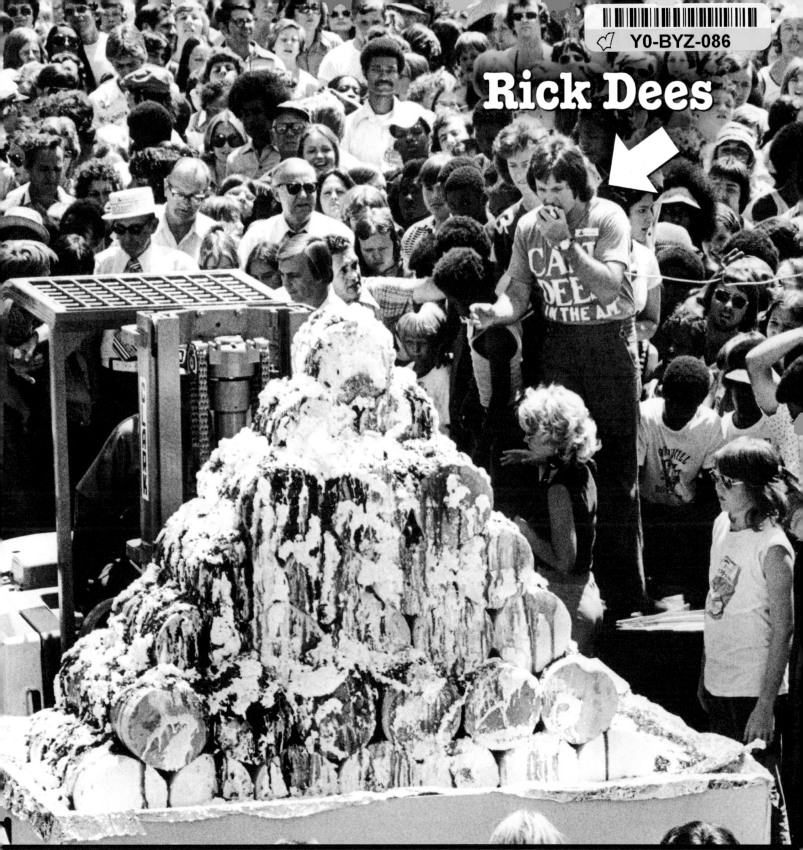

Rick Dees

super sundae & mr. dees   Photo credit: dave darnell

"World's Largest Ice Cream Sundae"
Memphis, Tennessee
June 1st, 1975

RICK DEES

All-Time Top

40

Greatest

DESSERTS

FOREWORD BY

WOLFGANG PUCK

To Julie and Kevin,
and thanks to my sister Patsy,
the greatest cake baker I have ever known.

Foreword

by Wolfgang Puck

My first introduction to Rick Dees was as surreal as what you might imagine when fine dining and Top 40 Radio cross paths. I was a young chef who recently arrived in Los Angeles. One day in the autumn of 1976 while I was actually cooking Peking Duck, the catchy hit "Disco Duck" came on the radio. What a crazy coincidence! I remembered the name of the man who wrote and recorded it.

Cut to winter 1982. I had just opened Spago on the Sunset Strip. Rick was the hottest radio personality in L.A. One night, he burst into my open kitchen and excitedly exclaimed, like he was announcing the latest hits, "Wolfgang! Your pizza is **number one!** And I'm going to tell the world!"

Sure enough, the next day, people kept coming up to me saying, "Rick Dees says your pizza is number one!" Rick and I have been friends ever since, and I quickly learned that we were both crazy about pastries and desserts.

One morning when I was a live guest on Rick's show, he sprang on me an avocado, pineapple, flour, three eggs, cinnamon, baking powder, baking soda, and salt—and challenged me to make something with them right there.

I created "Wolfgang's Wild Surprise." And it tasted pretty good.

For years now, Rick has continued enjoying the desserts in my restaurants, while also sharing with me his own sweet discoveries from his travels. So I'm delighted that he's sharing his favorites in this new book. Like Rick himself, they are approachable, down-to-earth, and great fun. You'll love every bite.

I have only one question: Rick, where is that recipe for my avocado-pineapple "Wolfgang's Wild Surprise?"

Rick Dees may be my best friend in the whole world, but he's no friend of my waistline!

It's worth it, though, because I'm fortunate enough to be one of the lead beneficiaries of his inexhaustible passion for finding and baking the world's finest desserts.

In fact, I may have myself to blame.

Rick was my college roommate back in the day, and the seeds for this book were sewn in my mother's North Carolina kitchen.

You see, it was during weekend trips home from UNC, with Rick happily in tow, that my mother, Barbara, encouraged him to learn the "art of dessert." Be careful what you wish for, Mom, because Rick took your inspiration entirely to heart and embarked on a lifelong search for dessert perfection. And now he's compiled his greatest finds in this outstanding edition.

My personal favorite? Well, there's his Old-Fashioned Apple Pie. Or maybe it's his Graham Cracker Toffee. But then again, there's his Classic Chocolate Cake. Now that I think of it, it's tough to come up with a single favorite. They're all so doggone good!

All these recipes and many more can be found in this fun, informative expression of Rick's culinary creativity. Believe me, if it's a dessert and it's in this book, you can't go wrong. So choose your own favorite—or favorites as the case may be.

Happy baking!

Ken Lowe
Chairman/CEO
Scripps Networks Interactive
HGTV, Food Network, Cooking Channel
DIY, Travel, GAC, and more

9

Introduction

I was the fattest kid in the 4th grade.

Never did I meet a peanut butter and jelly sandwich I didn't like. When I was six years old, I thought the only two letters in the alphabet were M&M.

This boy was genetically programmed for desserts.

But as I entered the 6th grade, the battle of sugar versus testosterone had begun, and testosterone emerged the victor as I shed 26 pounds, never to look back at that chubby kid again.

Playing sports became important to me, not only for the physical and social benefits, but also because the calories I burned left room for dessert. I was home again.

Being aware of the excitement desserts elicit with most people, I decided to impress my friends by baking my first pie. I'll never forget gathering fresh pecans from my grandmother's backyard in Goldsboro, North Carolina, and carefully following the recipe for fresh pecan pie.

As the pie emerged from its 350-degree cocoon, the fragrance was intoxicating. Add a dollop of vanilla ice cream, and I'm dating the head cheerleader.

From that first pie to the countless tastings through the years, I have been on a mission to find the greatest desserts of all time. My profession as an entertainer has taken me all over the world in search of desserts that after a single taste make one say, "Oh my, I have never tasted *anything* this good!"

The challenge of narrowing the list down to the "Top 40" desserts is daunting, but as you bake these simple recipes, just watch the responses on the faces of your guests after their first taste of one of these desserts.

You may even hear those magic words: "This dessert is **number one!**"

❧ Contents

Metric Equivalents

Measuring Cups

United States	Metric
1/4 cup	50 mL
1/3 cup	75 mL
1/2 cup	125 mL
1 cup	250 mL
1 1/4 cups	300 mL
1 1/3 cups	325 mL
1 1/2 cups	375 mL
2 cups	500 mL
2 1/4 cups	550 mL
2 1/3 cups	575 mL
2 1/2 cups	625 mL
3 cups	750 mL
3 1/4 cups	800 mL
3 1/3 cups	825 mL
3 1/2 cups	875 mL
4 cups	1 L
8 cups	2 L
16 cups	4 L
20 cups	8 L

Measuring Liquids

United States	Metric
1/2 oz	15 mL
1 oz	30 mL
1 1/2 oz	45 mL
2 oz	60 mL
2 1/2 oz	75 mL
3 oz	90 mL
3 1/2 oz	105 mL
4 oz	125 mL
4 1/2 oz	140 mL
5 oz	155 mL
5 1/2 oz	170 mL
6 oz	185 mL
6 1/2 oz	200 mL
7 oz	220 mL
7 1/2 oz	235 mL
8 oz	250 mL
16 oz	500 mL

Measuring Spoons

United States	Metric	United States	Metric
1/4 tsp	1 mL	1/4 Tbsp	5 mL
1/2 tsp	2 mL	1/2 Tbsp	10 mL
3/4 tsp	4 mL	3/4 Tbsp	15 mL
1 tsp	5 mL	1 Tbsp	20 mL
1 1/4 tsp	6 mL	1 1/4 Tbsp	25 mL
1 1/2 tsp	7 mL	1 1/2 Tbsp	30 mL
1 3/4 tsp	9 mL	1 3/4 Tbsp	35 mL
2 tsps	10 mL	2 Tbsp	40 mL
2 1/4 tsp	11 mL	2 1/4 Tbsp	45 mL
2 1/2 tsp	12 mL	2 1/2 Tbsp	50 mL
2 3/4 tsp	14 mL	2 3/4 Tbsp	55 mL
3 tsp	15 mL	3 Tbsp	60 mL

Measuring Dry Ingredients

United States	Metric	United States	Metric
1/2 oz	15 g	10 oz	315 g
1 oz (1/16 lb)	30 g	10 1/2 oz	330 g
1 1/2 oz	45 g	11 oz	350 g
2 oz	60 g	11 1/2 oz	365 g
2 1/2 oz	75 g	12 oz (3/4 lb)	375 g
3 oz	90 g	12 1/2 oz	390 g
3 1/2 oz	105 g	13 oz	410 g
4 oz (1/4 lb)	125 g	13 1/2 oz	425 g
4 1/2 oz	140 g	14 oz	440 g
5 oz	155 g	14 1/2 oz	455 g
5 1/2 oz	170 g	15 oz	470 g
6 oz	185 g	15 1/2 oz	485 g
6 1/2 oz	200 g	16 oz (1 lb)	500 g
7 oz	220 g	24 oz (1 1/2 lbs)	750 g
7 1/2 oz	235 g	2 lbs	1 kg
8 oz (1/2 lb)	250 g	3 lbs	1.5 kg
8 1/2 oz	265 g	4 lbs	2 kg
9 oz	280 g	5 lbs	2.5 kg
9 1/2 oz	295 g		

Cooking/Oven Temperatures

	Fahrenheit	Celsius
Freezing Water	32°F	0°C
Room Temperature	68°F	20°C
Boiling Water	212°F	100°C
Baking Temperatures	325°F	160°C
	350°F	180°C
	375°F	190°C
	400°F	200°C
	425°F	220°C
	450°F	230°C

Aunt Mary's Pumpkin Pie

(page 27)

✐ The #1 Pie Crust

The perfect crust is the foundation for every great pie. This crust is the absolute best, making enough dough for a superbly flaky 9-inch double crust pie. The frozen crust will keep in your freezer for up to four weeks.

Once the crust is in the pie plate, fork-prick the bottom of the crust several times before putting it in the oven.

Directions for Preparation

1. With about 2 quick pulses, process the flour, salt, and sugar in food processor until combined.

2. Add the butter and lard to the mixture and process for 15 seconds until the dough just starts to collect in uneven clumps. It will resemble cottage cheese curds with no uncoated flour remaining.

3. Scrape the bowl with a rubber spatula and redistribute the dough evenly. Add the remaining cup of flour and give the dough 4 to 6 quick pulses until the mixture is distributed around the bowl and the dough mass has been broken up.

4. Empty the dough into a medium-sized bowl. Sprinkle the vodka and ice water over the dough.

5. With a rubber spatula, use a folding motion to mix and press down the dough until it is slightly tacky and sticks together.

6. Divide the dough into 2 equal balls and flatten each into a 4-inch disk. Cover each dough ball with plastic wrap and refrigerate at least 45 minutes until ready to use.

Chef's Note

When using frozen #1 Pie Crust, you should prebake it to prevent the pie from having a soggy bottom. Let the frozen crust thaw just enough so you can prick it with a fork, then prebake the semi-frozen crust for about 10 minutes at 425°F. Pour in the filling and bake per recipe instructions.

If not shielded during final baking, the exposed prebaked crust may get too brown. Use pie shields or cut thin strips of aluminum foil to cover the exposed crust.

Yield: Makes one 9-inch double crust

Prep Time: 10 to 15 minutes

Chill Time: 30 to 40 minutes

Total Time: 60 minutes

Ingredients

The #1 Pie Crust

2 1/2 cups all-purpose flour

1/2 teaspoon table salt

2 tablespoons sugar

12 tablespoons (1 1/2 sticks) salted butter, cold and cut into 1/4-inch pieces

1/2 cup lard,* cold and cut into 1/4-inch pieces

1/4 cup water, ice cold

1/4 cup vodka, cold

Chef's Note

Vodka binds with the gluten keeping the dough moist and flaky. Its alcohol content evaporates during baking.

Apple cider vinegar can be substituted for vodka and will make your crust extra tender.

* There is a difference between lard and shortening: Lard makes a better crust.

When Ready to Use

1. Remove 1 dough disk from the refrigerator and roll out onto a lightly floured work surface. Lightly dust both the rolling pin and top of the dough with flour. Roll into a 12-inch circle about 1/4 inch thick and about 2 inches larger than the pie plate.

2. Roll the dough loosely around a rolling pin and unroll into a prepared pie plate, leaving at least a 1-inch overhang. Ease the dough into the pie plate by gently lifting the edge of the dough with one hand while pressing into the plate bottom with the other hand.

Mastering the Perfect Pie Crust ⟣

3. Trim off excess dough with a paring knife, leaving dough about 1/2 inch wider than the diameter of the dish. Reserve remaining dough for decoration.

4. Flute the dough by placing a finger against the edge of the pastry. Using the thumb and index finger of the other hand, press the dough around the finger. Continue around the rest of the dough's edge. Chill the prepared crust in the refrigerator for 30 to 40 minutes until ready to fill with prepared pie filling.

The number one secret to the perfect pie crust is to keep the dough chilled. Keeping the dough cool and handling it minimally will keep your dough rich, flaky, and perfect for any recipe.

～ Rick's Old-Fashioned Apple Pie

Of all the delicious fruits on earth, the succulent apple has been the most revered.

Even at the dawn of mankind in the Garden of Eden, the apple was impossible to resist.

I vividly remember my first irresistible taste of old-fashioned apple pie. Visiting my grandmother, Helen Dees, in Myrtle Beach, South Carolina, my mom took me by my young five-year-old hand and we walked up the front steps. The door swung open and we were met by Grandma's smiling face and a pleasant fragrance I had not experienced until that day.

I was curiously attracted by the scent and blurted out, "Mama, what smells so good?"

She replied, "Your grandmother has just baked a fresh apple pie! Let's see if she'll give you a slice."

I will always remember what happened next.

Warm, fresh apple pie.

Cold, frosty vanilla ice cream.

One spoon.

After three swift bites, I was so excited about the taste of apple pie that I jumped up and down and shook my hips like I had swallowed a jackhammer.

The secret to all great pies is the crust. There are so many times I have tasted the filling of a pie only to be disappointed by a crust that tastes like cardboard. Such is not the case with this award-winning apple pie. It's simple, with just enough sweetness from a couple of secrets you are about to discover. These two secrets answer to the names of lard and butter.

There seems to be a perfect texture for apples that are cooked just enough in an apple pie. So follow me now to that blissful world of Granny Smith.

Rick's Old-Fashioned Apple Pie ∽

Yield: Makes one 9-inch pie

Prep Time: 30 minutes

Crust Chill Time: 60 minutes

Total Time: 90 minutes

🥄 Ingredients

Pie Crust

One double crust using
The #1 Pie Crust
(page 19)

Apple Filling

1 cup granulated sugar

3/4 cup light brown sugar

4 tablespoons flour

1 teaspoon cinnamon

1 teaspoon nutmeg

1/2 teaspoon salt

2 tablespoons freshly
squeezed lemon juice

6 to 7 apples,
sliced & peeled

4 tablespoons salted butter

2 tablespoons vanilla extract

👨‍🍳 Chef's Note

For this classic favorite,
I like to use either
Golden Delicious or
Granny Smith apples.
Golden Delicious never fail
to add the perfect flavor,
while Granny Smith apples
break down less
when they cook.

Directions for Pie Crust

1. Preheat oven to 350°F.

2. Make pie crust according to directions.

3. Fit pie crust into a 9-inch deep-dish pie plate and flute the pie shell edges. Chill crust in refrigerator for 30 to 40 minutes while preparing the Apple Filling.

Directions for Apple Filling

1. Combine sugars, flour, cinnamon, nutmeg, salt, and lemon juice. Mix lightly, then add the apples.

2. Melt butter, then add to the apple filling.

3. Place the filling in a saucepan. Add vanilla extract and cook at medium-low heat for about 10 to12 minutes to pre-soften the apples. Remove from stove and mix with a fork or spoon.

4. Pour filling into the pie shell. Cover the pie either fully with a second crust or with a latticework crust.

5. Bake at 350°F for 30 to 40 minutes until crust is brown and the apples are tender.

Serve warm with a hearty scoop of your favorite vanilla bean ice cream.

Spectacular!

☙ Aunt Mary's Pumpkin Pie

Let's get one thing straight: there is no Aunt Mary…but if I had just said, "Delicious Pumpkin Pie," you would've turned the page.

And now, inspired by a fictitious Aunt Mary, here's a simple recipe that will make your guests and friends say, "How did you do this? I've never tasted pumpkin pie like this!" And isn't that what baking is all about?

Most of us associate pumpkin pie with seasonal events, but you'll want to serve this one on a regular basis. Don't forget to include homemade whipped cream or a scoop of the finest vanilla ice cream you can find!

Chef's Note

In a hurry? Simply put all your pumpkin filling ingredients in the blender and blend well for about 2 minutes. Pour the mixture into your chilled prepared pie crust and bake. Aunt Mary won't mind.

Aunt Mary's Pumpkin Pie ✍

Yield: Makes one 9-inch pie

Prep Time: 30 minutes

Crust Chill Time: 60 minutes

Total Time: 90 minutes

🥄 Ingredients

Pie Crust

One double crust using
The #1 Pie Crust
(page 19)

Pumpkin Filling

1 cup granulated sugar

1/2 teaspoon salt

1/2 teaspoon cinnamon

1/2 teaspoon nutmeg

1/2 teaspoon ground cloves

1 15-ounce can of pumpkin

2 large eggs, beaten

1 tablespoon vanilla extract

3 tablespoons salted butter,
melted

1 cup evaporated milk
or half & half

Directions for Pie Crust

1. Preheat oven to 450°F.

2. Make pie crust according to directions.

3. Fit pie crust into a 9-inch deep-dish pie plate. Chill the crust a second time for 20 to 30 minutes. Set aside.

We recommend making the full pie crust recipe and freezing half for future use, or using the remainder for pie decoration. No prebaking is necessary for Aunt Mary's Pumpkin Pie.

Directions for Pumpkin Filling

1. Mix together the dry ingredients of sugar, salt, cinnamon, nutmeg, and cloves.

2. Add pumpkin, beaten eggs, vanilla extract, melted butter, and evaporated milk (or half & half) into the dry mixture, then beat on medium speed for about 2 minutes.

3. Pour the mixture into the chilled pie crust. Cover pie edges with aluminum foil strips or pie crust shields to prevent pie crust edges from burning.

4. Bake at 450°F for 10 minutes, then reduce to 350°F and bake for 40 to 50 minutes or until a toothpick or sharp knife comes out moist and almost clean.

Serve warm with a hearty scoop of your favorite vanilla bean ice cream or fresh whipped cream.

It's "Dees-licious!"

❧ Greatest Lemon Meringue Pie

My first experience with lemon meringue pie was in Jacksonville, Florida.

There were some lemon trees growing near our little home down by the St. John's River. One day my mother stopped the car in front of our neighbor's front yard and fetched four lemons that had fallen off the tree and rolled out onto the sidewalk.

Ann Dees, lovingly known to her family and friends as "The Mouth of the South," blurted out in her unique Southern drawl, "Son, don't worry; they'll never miss them!"

I'll never forget the pie she made with those lemons.

She said the recipe was handed down from her mother, May Smith Dees, and I have taken the liberty to use this recipe as the template of the greatest lemon meringue pie you will ever consume. The recipe that follows is a combination of 15 different lemon meringue pie recipes that I have tirelessly tasted in my quest for the greatest lemon meringue pie.

The filling, the meringue, and the crust all work in concert to slap your taste buds around and have them love it. And isn't that what taste buds are meant to do?

Greatest Lemon Meringue Pie ✍

Yield: Makes one 10-inch pie

Prep Time: 30 minutes

Crust Chill Time: 60 minutes

Total Time: 90 minutes

♨ Ingredients

Pie Crust

One double crust using
The #1 Pie Crust
(page 19)

Lemon Filling

1 1/2 cups granulated sugar

2 level tablespoons cornstarch

1/3 cup flour

1/4 teaspoon salt

1 3/4 cups water, boiling

4 egg yolks, beaten

1/2 cup freshly squeezed
lemon juice
(from 2 to 3 lemons)

3 heaping tablespoons
lemon zest
(from 3 to 4 lemons)

1 tablespoon vanilla extract

4 tablespoons salted butter,
softened

Meringue

8 egg whites,
room temperature

1 1/3 cups granulated sugar

1/2 teaspoon salt

1 teaspoon cream of tartar

1 1/3 tablespoon
vanilla extract

Directions for Pie Crust

1. Preheat oven to 350°F.

2. Make pie crust according to directions. Put into pie plate and chill 20 to 30 minutes. Save any remaining pie dough to use later.

3. Remove prepared pie plate from refrigerator and blind-bake crust (partially baking the pie crust before adding the filling). Line pie with parchment, snugging the lining right up against the edges and sides of the pie. Fill pie with pie weights (dry beans or rice work great), making sure they cover the bottom of the pie and press up against the sides. Bake at 350°F for 10 to 12 minutes until edges are barely golden.

4. Remove crust from oven and remove pie weights and parchment. Poke small holes in the bottom of the pie crust with a fork. Bake for an additional 3 to 5 minutes until crust is golden. The bottom crust will puff a bit as it bakes, but will deflate again after you remove the pie from the oven.

5. Remove from oven. Set aside.

Directions for Lemon Filling

1. Combine the four dry ingredients of sugar, cornstarch, flour, and salt into a saucepan. Gradually add the boiling water while stirring. Cook the sugar mixture on medium heat until it begins to boil, stirring constantly. The sugar mixture should begin to thicken. Remove from heat.

2. Combine the egg yolks, lemon juice, and lemon zest. Stir into the saucepan containing the sugar mixture. Return to heat and stir constantly until mixture returns to a boil and again thickens.

3. Stir in the vanilla extract and butter while continuing to stir and scrape the bottom of the saucepan until the mixture thickens once more. Boil 2 to 3 minutes, stirring constantly. Remove from heat.

4. Spoon filling into the prebaked pie crust.

Directions for Meringue

1. Beat egg whites in mixing bowl until foamy.

2. Gradually beat in the sugar and cream of tartar until stiff peaks form. Add vanilla extract and continue beating well on high speed until stiff peaks hold.

3. Immediately spread meringue onto the warm lemon filling, sealing the edges to the pastry.

4. Bake pie at 350°F for a few minutes until the meringue is golden brown.

Chef's Note

1. Weeping is when syrup from the meringue puddles from the bottom of the meringue creating a slippery layer between the curd and the meringue topping. To avoid this, do not cool the curd after placing it in the pie crust. Adding the meringue to a hot or warm curd cooks the meringue from the bottom and helps bond the two layers.

2. Don't cut the pie before it's fully cooled. If you cut the pie too soon, the curd will break and your meringue could fall. For best results, make sure the pie plate is cool to the touch when you place your hand on the bottom center. Once it has cooled completely, it's time to dig in.

3. It's OK to want seconds.

↝ Pecan Pie

The pecan is one of the most flavorful nuts on planet Earth. It has a soft texture with a hint of butter and natural oil that make it a willing partner in any recipe.

A simple pecan pie is easy to make, easy to bake, and a great dessert to prepare when you're running short on time.

As you can see from the ingredients, there are only eight. The key that unlocks the flavor is the vanilla married to the butter and pecans.

This pie can stand on its own. You'll go nuts over it.

Chef's Note
Perfect pecan pie begins with great nuts.
To bring out a nuttier flavor, pan roast them
for 5 to 8 minutes at 350°F until you can
smell the pecan aroma.

↝ Pies | 35

Pecan Pie ～

Yield: Makes one 9-inch pie

Prep Time: 20-30 minutes

Crust Chill Time: 30 minutes

Total Time: 90 minutes

⚖ Ingredients

Pie Crust

One double crust using
Amazingly Easy & Fast
Pie Crust
(page 219)

Pecan Filling

3 large eggs

1 1/2 teaspoons vanilla extract

3 tablespoons salted butter,
softened

1/2 cup granulated sugar

2 tablespoons flour

1/2 teaspoon salt

1 cup light corn syrup

1 cup pecans,
lightly toasted

Directions for Pie Crust

1. Make pie crust according to Mix directions. Add the additional butter to Mix, per recipe instructions.

2. Roll out dough to fit pie plate, saving any remaining pie dough to use later. Chill for 30 minutes.

Directions for Pecan Filling

1. Preheat oven to 400°F.

2. Beat the eggs thoroughly, then add the vanilla extract.

3. Melt the butter and add it into the mixture, then fold in the sugar, flour, and salt.

4. Add the light corn syrup, then the toasted pecans. Use the nuts whole, in halves, or chopped, whichever you prefer. It's an equal substitution: 1 cup whole pecans equals 1 cup chopped. Blend well.

5. Fill the pie crust with the pecan filling.

6. Bake at 400°F for the first 8 minutes, then reduce heat to 350°F and bake an additional 35 to 40 minutes.

Be sure to allow your pie to cool completely before cutting. A warm pie will not be set, and your slices will not hold a clean edge.

Go over the top and serve with butter pecan ice cream.

Tastes wonderful!

There was a group of immigrants over 200 years ago who called themselves the "Shakers."

Word has it that the Shakers got their name from meetings where a man would stand on one side of the room and a woman would stand on the other, and instead of dancing or touching one another, they would start shaking, gyrating, and trembling their bodies in an effort to shake off any physical desires they might have for the opposite sex.

Because they didn't follow through with the shaking, the Shakers thinned out quickly. But they did leave behind a legacy of fine furniture making and wonderful baking.

This pie is the purest complement to a lemon you could ever make. The tartness of the whole lemon combined with the sweetness gives one of the most natural flavors you'll ever experience.

Allow me to introduce you to Shaker Lemon Pie.

Shaker Lemon Pie ✍

Yield: Makes one 9-inch pie

Prep Time: 30 minutes

Crust Chill Time: 60 minutes

Macerating Time: 4 to 24 hours

Total Time: 1 1/2 to 24 hours

⚖ Ingredients

Pie Crust

One double crust using
The #1 Pie Crust
(page 19)

Lemon Filling

2 large lemons

2 cups granulated sugar

1/4 teaspoon salt

1 tablespoon vanilla extract

5 eggs, well-beaten
(4 for filling, 1 for egg wash)

3 tablespoons salted butter,
melted

2 tablespoons raw sugar

👨‍🍳 Chef's Note

If you don't have a good slicer handy, here's another tool that will make thinly slicing the lemons much easier: the freezer. Popping lemons into the freezer for about 15 minutes firms them up for better slicing, which is best accomplished with a serrated knife.

Directions for Pie Crust

1. Make pie crust according to directions.

2. Fit pie crust into a 9-inch deep-dish pie plate. Chill crust thoroughly in refrigerator for 30 to 40 minutes while preparing the lemon filling.

Directions for Lemon Filling

1. Put 2 large lemons in the freezer for about 15 minutes. (Cold lemons are easier to grate and cut.)

2. Remove lemons from freezer and finely grate only the yellow rind (not the white) of each lemon onto a plate.

3. Using a sharp serrated knife, cut the end knobs off of each lemon. Slice each lemon into razor-thin slices.

4. Cut off the white part (pith) and remove the seed, leaving just the pulp.

5. Cut the pulp into quarters and put into a bowl with the yellow grated peel.

6. Add the sugar, salt, and vanilla extract to the lemon pulp and grated lemon peel. Cover and let stand from 4 hours to overnight on counter or in refrigerator.

The longer the filling is allowed to macerate (or soak), the more the sugar permeates into the citrus, adding sweetness and flavor. Stir mixture occasionally to further blend.

Prepare to Bake

1. Preheat oven to 425°F.

2. Whisk 4 eggs well. Add the eggs and the 3 tablespoons of melted butter to the lemon mixture and stir until thoroughly combined.

3. Remove prepared chilled pie crust from the refrigerator and blind-bake in 425°F oven for 10 minutes, or until crust is almost beige but not even close to brown.

4. Remove crust from oven and turn the lemon mixture into the pie crust. Cover with a top crust, sealing the edges by crimping them with your fingers. Slice a few slits in the top of the crust near the center of the pie.

5. Make an egg wash: Whisk egg, adding a splash of water. Brush the egg wash all over the top crust. Sprinkle crust evenly with 2 tablespoons of raw sugar.

6. Bake at 400°F for 15 minutes, then reduce heat to 350°F and bake for an additional 40 minutes or until pie is golden brown, center is not jiggly, and a knife inserted near the edge of the pie comes out clean.

Remove pie from oven and allow to cool on a wire rack. The longer it cools, the more it will set up, making it much easier to slice for serving.

If you're looking for a dessert that enhances any meal, then here it is: Chess Pie. You'll even impress yourself with the ease of assembly and baking.

Most of the time you'll want to add a scoop of your favorite vanilla ice cream with the pie, and if you do, I'll look the other way.

When Chess Pie is served slightly warm, its texture and taste are most inviting. It's simple—try it!

Chess Pie ✎

Yield: Makes one 9-inch pie
Prep Time: 20 minutes
Crust Chill Time: 30 minutes
Total Time: 90 minutes

🥄 Ingredients

Pie Crust

One double crust using
Amazingly Easy & Fast
Pie Crust
(page 219)

Filling

1 1/2 cups granulated sugar

4 eggs

1/2 cup (1 stick) salted butter, melted

1 tablespoon distilled white vinegar

1 tablespoon yellow cornmeal

1 teaspoon vanilla extract

5 tablespoons milk

👨‍🍳 Chef's Note

The filling will finish baking as it cools, so resist the temptation to leave the pie in the oven until the filling looks fully set. Too much time in the oven can result in a cracked custard once the pie cools.

Directions for Pie Crust

1. Make pie crust according to packaged Mix directions. Add the additional butter, per recipe instructions.

2. Roll out dough to fit pie plate, saving any remaining pie dough to use later. Chill for 30 minutes.

Directions for Filling

1. Preheat oven to 350°F.

2. Combine sugar and eggs with a wire whisk, mixing well.

3. Add melted butter, vinegar, cornmeal, vanilla extract, and milk to the mixture, stirring well.

4. Pour mixture into the prepared chilled pie crust.

5. Bake at 350°F for 40 minutes or until the center barely jiggles.

Let pie set for one hour. This allows ample time for the pie to properly set before serving.

From the early days of horse racing, as the steeds crossed the finish line, the excitement was heightened by the anticipation that all in attendance would be enjoying fresh Sweetbrier Pie.

The morsels of chocolate, fresh nuts, and a buttery filling will make you want to race down the track ahead of the horses.

The flavors don't fight each other for the finish line—they all finish in a tie.

Chef's Note

After baking, allow this pie to fully cool to room temperature. Although it can be served warm, it's best cooled when it is completely set.

Sweetbrier Pie

Yield: Makes one 9-inch pie

Prep Time: 15 minutes

Crust Chill Time: 60 minutes

Total Time: 1 hour 15 minutes

Ingredients

Pie Crust

One double crust using
The #1 Pie Crust
(page 19)

Filling

4 eggs, slightly beaten

1 cup granulated sugar

1 cup light brown sugar

2 cups chocolate chips,
melted

2 cups pecans, chopped

1 cup (2 sticks) salted butter,
melted

2 teaspoons vanilla extract

1 cup flour

Chef's Note

The chocolate chips may be
left to your preference:
semisweet, milk chocolate,
or bittersweet chocolate.
For a richer flavor, consider a
mix instead of just one type.

Directions for Pie Crust

1. Make pie crust according to directions, reserving half for future use.

2. Fit pie crust into a 9-inch deep-dish pie plate. Chill crust in refrigerator 30 to 40 minutes while preparing filling.

Directions for Filling

1. Preheat oven to 350°F.

2. Combine the eggs, sugars, chocolate chips, pecans, butter, and vanilla extract, adding the flour last. Mix well.

3. Pour mixture into the chilled pie crust. Bake at 350°F for 30 minutes.

Allow to thoroughly cool (at least 2 hours) before slicing to allow the pie to fully firm up.

Along the shores of Miami Beach and into the Gulf, your journey across the southernmost highway of the United States isn't complete unless you stop in the Florida Keys and enjoy the original Key Lime Pie.

This version of Key Lime Pie gets the highest marks from native Floridians and visitors from around the world. It's not green like the Key lime, because the color green works for the lime but not for the dessert. Studies confirm this odd fact.

You'll notice that the zest of the lime adds a flavorful reminder of the freshness of the Florida Keys.

Does it taste fresher with the grated lime peel? Yes. Is there a harsh aftertaste? No. Will I stop interviewing myself now? Yes.

Chef's Note

Here's a quick trick to help make juicing limes easier: Microwave the whole, uncut fruit for 15 seconds or soak the whole fruit in warm water for several minutes. Using a citrus reamer (or a fork) will then extract the most juice possible.

Key Lime Pie ❦

Yield: Makes one 9-inch pie
Prep Time: 30 minutes
Crust Chill Time: 60 minutes
Total Time: 90 minutes

🥄 Ingredients

Pie Crust

1 double crust using
The #1 Pie Crust
(page 19)

Filling

1/3 cup cornstarch
1 1/2 cups granulated sugar
1/4 teaspoon salt
1 cup water
4 egg yolks, slightly beaten
(save egg whites for
the meringue)
2/3 cup sweetened
condensed milk
1/3 cup Key lime juice
2 tablespoons grated
lime peel
3 tablespoons salted butter
1 teaspoon vanilla extract

Meringue

8 egg whites,
room temperature
1/2 teaspoon cream of tartar
1 cup sugar
4 teaspoons vanilla extract

Directions for Pie Crust

1. Preheat oven to 350°F.

2. Make pie crust according to directions, reserving half for future use. Fit into 9-inch pie plate and chill or 20 to 30 minutes.

3. Remove from refrigerator and blind-bake (prebaking the crust with pie weights). Bake at 350°F for 10 to 12 minutes until crust is firm.

4. Remove pie weights and poke small holes in the bottom of the pie crust with a fork, then bake for an additional 3 to 5 minutes until crust is golden.

5. Remove from oven. Set aside.

Directions for Filling

1. Preheat oven to 400°F.

2. In a small saucepan, combine cornstarch, sugar, and salt. Gradually add the water, stirring until smooth.

3. Over medium heat, bring the mixture to a boil, stirring constantly. Boil 1 minute while stirring.

4. Remove from heat. Quickly stir half of the mixture into the egg yolks and condensed milk, mixing well. Return mixture to saucepan.

5. Over medium heat, return the mixture to boiling and boil for 30 seconds.

6. Remove from heat. Stir in lime juice, lime peel, butter, and vanilla extract until well combined. Pour immediately into the prepared pie crust. Allow filling to cool as you prepare the meringue.

Directions for Meringue

1. In a medium-sized bowl beat the egg whites and cream of tartar at medium speed until soft peaks form when the beater is raised.

2. Gradually beat in the sugar 2 tablespoons at a time, mixing well after each addition.

3. Add 2 teaspoons of vanilla extract, beating until stiff peaks are formed when beater is raised.

4. Spread the meringue over the filling, being sure to seal to the edges of the pie crust.

5. Bake at 400°F for 7 to 9 minutes or until meringue is golden.

Cool on wire rack away from drafts for about an hour before serving. Serve chilled or at room temperature—Key Lime Pie is tasty either way.

This is one *dees-licious* pie!

Chef's Note

The refreshing taste of the pie (and its sliceable texture) depend on the pie being set all the way through. This makes the last step in making Key Lime Pie the hardest: waiting as it chills in the refrigerator.

Key Lime Pie
(page 51)

Notice the word "fresh." Fresh coconut adds a dimension to this pie that kicks it to a higher level.

Do not confuse this coconut pie with coconut cream pie bought in the frigid sections of a supermarket. There's a reason they live on those back shelves and wait for long periods of time yearning to be purchased.

Fresh Coconut Pie is an entirely different experience. The flavor of coconut is enhanced when its partner is sweet, so the sugar and coconut together make a perfect marriage.

Here you go: Fresh Coconut Pie.

Chef's Note

To ensure the dried coconut fully softens as the pie bakes, soak it in cultured buttermilk for 15 minutes before adding it to the custard.

Fresh Coconut Pie ✑

Yield: Makes one 9-inch pie

Prep Time: 30 minutes

Crust Chill Time: 60 minutes

Total Time: 90 minutes

⚘ Ingredients

Pie Crust

1 double crust using
The #1 Pie Crust
(page 19)

Coconut Filling

1/2 cup (1 stick) salted butter

1 1/4 cups granulated sugar

1/4 cup all-purpose flour

4 eggs

3/4 cup cultured buttermilk

1 tablespoon vanilla extract

1 1/4 cups coconut,
shredded

Directions for Pie Crust

1. Preheat oven to 375°F.

2. Make pie crust according to directions, reserving half for future use.

3. Roll out pie crust in a 9-inch pie plate, then flute the edges with the excess dough hanging over the edge of the pie plate. Line the pie crust with double-thickness foil.

4. Bake at 375°F for 10 minutes. Remove foil and bake for an additional 4 to 6 minutes or until crust is light brown. Remove from oven to cool and set aside.

Directions for Coconut Filling

1. Reduce oven heat to 350°F.

2. In a medium-sized saucepan, melt the butter over medium-low heat. Stir in the sugar and flour, then remove from heat and set aside.

3. In a medium-sized bowl, whisk the eggs well. Add the cultured buttermilk and vanilla extract, whisking until the mixture is just combined.

4. Gradually whisk the buttermilk mixture into the butter mixture, blending until smooth.

5. Stir the coconut into the mixture until well combined.

6. Pour the mixture into the prepared pie crust.

7. Cover the pie shell edges with foil to prevent overbrowning.

8. Bake at 350°F for 30 minutes, then remove the foil. Bake pie for an additional 10 minutes or until top of pie is golden brown and a knife inserted near the pie's center comes out clean.

Allow to cool fully (about 4 hours) and serve at room temperature. If served from refrigerator, allow chilled pie to stand at room temperature for an hour before serving.

⌘ Boston Cream Pie

After the Boston Tea Party when they realized they'd thrown all their tea into the harbor, the Patriots of the New World knew they had to create something to make up for their loss.

Boston Cream Pie was the celebrated result.

The custard filling is vital to the enjoyment of any Boston Cream Pie, and the chocolate adds a crown of decadent delight. The moist cake is the perfect buffer between the flavors of chocolate and custard.

To paraphrase Paul Revere: "The British are coming, and they're demanding Boston Cream Pie!"

Chef's Note
Chill the cake in the refrigerator for 10 to 15 minutes before serving to firm up the cake and make slicing easier.

Boston Cream Pie ❦

Yield: Makes one 8-inch
or 9-inch pie

Prep Time: 20 minutes

Total Time: 2 hours 45 minutes

🥄 Ingredients

Golden Butter Cake

1 cup cake flour

1 teaspoon baking powder

1/4 teaspoon salt

3 tablespoons salted butter

4 tablespoons milk

2 tablespoons vanilla extract

5 eggs, room temperature

3/4 cup (12 tablespoons)
granulated sugar

Boston Cream Pie
Custard Filling

2 cups whole milk

7 large egg yolks

1/2 cup granulated sugar

1/4 teaspoon salt

1/4 cup cornstarch,
sifted

1 tablespoon vanilla extract

2 tablespoons salted butter

Chocolate Glaze

1 cup heavy cream

1/4 cup light corn syrup

8 ounces bittersweet
chocolate (two 4-ounce
bars, 60 percent cacao
recommended)

2 tablespoons vanilla extract

Directions for Golden Butter Cake

1. Preheat oven to 350°F.

2. Butter and flour two 8-inch or two 9-inch cake pans,
   covering the bottoms of the pans with parchment paper.

3. Sift flour, baking powder, and salt. Set aside.

4. In a small saucepan, melt the butter with milk over low heat.
   Remove from heat, then add the vanilla extract, stirring well.
   Cover and keep warm.

5. Separate the egg whites and yolks of 3 eggs into two bowls.
   Crack the remaining 2 whole eggs into the yolk bowl.
   Beat the 3 egg whites until foamy.

6. Gradually add 6 tablespoons of sugar to the egg whites,
   continuing to beat until soft and moist peaks form.
   Take care not to overbeat.

7. Add the remaining 6 tablespoons of sugar to the egg yolks
   and beat on medium-high speed for 5 minutes until
   the eggs are very thick and pale in color.

8. Fold the egg whites into the egg yolk mixture. Sprinkle flour
   over the egg mixture, folding very gently with a large rubber
   spatula. Continue adding flour, folding until batter shows
   no trace of the flour and whites and whole eggs are evenly
   mixed.

9. Pour batter into prepared baking pans.

10. Bake at 350°F for 20 minutes if using 8-inch cake pans, or
    16 minutes if using 9-inch cake pans. Cake tops should be
    firm and spring back when touched.

11. Remove from oven, cool 10 minutes, then run a knife around
    the pan perimeter to loosen the cake. Cover pan with a
    large plate and invert pan to remove the cake from the pan.
    Peel off the parchment, then re-invert cake from plate onto
    a cooling rack. Repeat with second cake layer.

Directions for Boston Cream Pie Custard Filling

1. In a small saucepan, heat milk until warm but not simmering.

2. In a separate saucepan, whisk egg yolks, sugar, and salt together for 3 minutes until the mixture is thick and lemon colored. Add cornstarch, whisking to combine.

3. Slowly whisk the hot milk into the mixture, blending well. Cook over medium-low heat for 10 minutes, whisking constantly until the mixture thickens to a pudding consistency.

4. Remove from heat and stir in the vanilla extract and butter, blending until butter is melted.

5. Transfer custard filling to a container and cover with plastic wrap, directly touching the surface of the filling to prevent skin from forming. Refrigerate until firm.

Directions for Chocolate Glaze

1. In a medium-sized saucepan, bring heavy cream and corn syrup to a full simmer over medium heat. Remove from heat.

2. Add chocolate and vanilla extract, stirring very gently until mixture is smooth. Allow to cool until tepid. To speed up cooling, refrigerate briefly and stir every few minutes to ensure even cooling.

Directions for Assembling Boston Cream Pie

NOTE: To make a 4-layer Boston Cream Pie, use a serrated knife to split each of the 2 cooled sponge cakes into 4 layers of equal height. Proceed with assembly.

1. While the chocolate glaze is cooling, place the bottom cake layer on waxed paper. Carefully spoon cooled custard filling evenly over the cake, spreading to the cake edges.

2. Place the second cake layer on top of the custard filling, making sure the layers line up properly. If making a 4-layer pie, repeat addition of custard layers.

3. Pour the chocolate glaze over the middle of the top layer of cake, allowing it to flow down the sides. Use a spatula if necessary to completely coat the cake.

Allow 1 hour for the glaze to fully set before serving.

ဏ Sundae Pie

Picture this: You crave a freshly made sundae with hand-churned ice cream, but you don't want to eat it in front of your friends.

A perfect solution is Sundae Pie. It tastes like a sundae, it slices like a pie, and everybody will want a large wedge.

Drizzle a little extra chocolate sauce from the recipe for the World's #1 Hot Fudge Sauce that's coming up.

I think you're going to like this one. This "Deesert" could bring sweet and salty tears to your eyes.

Chef's Note

Can't wait for the World's #1 Hot Fudge Sauce?
Flip ahead to page 179 for the recipe.

Sundae Pie ✑

Yield: Makes one 9-inch pie

Prep Time: 30 minutes

Total Time: 60 to 90 minutes

🥄 Ingredients

Chocolate Cookie Crumb Crust

7 tablespoons salted butter, softened

1/2 cup granulated sugar

1/4 cup brown sugar

1 cup all-purpose flour, sifted

1/2 cup Dutch-processed cocoa powder, sifted

1/2 teaspoon salt

3 tablespoons salted butter, melted and cooled

Ice Cream Filling

8 cups (2 quarts) French vanilla ice cream

Whipped Cream Topping

1 cup heavy cream

2 tablespoons confectioners' sugar

Caramel Sauce

1 1/2 cups Caramel Sauce (page 217)

Directions for Chocolate Cookie Crumb Crust

1. Preheat oven to 350°F.

2. Line a baking sheet with parchment paper and set aside.

3. In a mixing bowl, cream the butter and sugars for 4 to 5 minutes on medium to high speed, scraping down the sides of the bowl as needed.

4. Turn off the mixer and add the flour, cocoa powder, and salt. Mix well on low, taking care to scrape down the sides and bottom as needed. The mixture will feel very dry and crumbly.

5. Pour the mixture onto the prepared baking sheet, spreading it out so the mixture is approximately 1/2 inch thick.

6. Bake at 350°F for 10 minutes, rotating the pan after 5 minutes.

7. Remove from the oven and stir the crumble around, moving the outer edges into the center to prevent burning. Continue to bake for an additional 10 minutes, then remove from the oven. Allow crumble to cool completely in the pan.

8. In a food processor, pulse the crumble for 20 seconds until it is pulverized into small uniform crumbs.

9. Transfer the crumbs into a bowl, then stir in the melted butter. The crumbs will feel slightly wet.

10. Using your fingers, press the crumbs into the bottom and sides of a 9-inch pie plate or springform pan, forming a uniform crust. Refrigerate for 20 minutes before filling.

Directions for Ice Cream Filling

1. Allow ice cream to sit out of the freezer for 15 to 20 minutes, until the sides look damp but the center is still quite firm.

2. Put the ice cream into a mixing bowl and mix until it is smooth but still very frozen (not drippy or melting).

3. Pour the ice cream into the prepared pie crust, smoothing the top of the pie so it domes in the middle.

4. Place the pie in the freezer for at least 1 hour to refreeze.

Directions for Caramel Sauce

Make Caramel Sauce (page 217) according to directions.

Directions for Assembling Sundae Pie

1. Whip the heavy cream and the confectioners' sugar together until soft peaks form. Place in a piping bag fitted with a fluted tip if desired, and pipe rosettes or drop dollops of whipped cream around the edges of the pie.

2. Drizzle caramel over the top of pie, adding chocolate chips if desired. Serve immediately.

≈ Apple Cobbler

Apple Cobbler satisfies the quest for a dessert that goes with almost any meal. This cobbler can be baked in a dish or in individual servings, and you'll notice it's easy to prepare and difficult to mess up.

The subtle nuances of cinnamon, nutmeg, and butter make the apples spring to life—you can't beat the fragrance of this wonderful dessert!

Let's do it!

Chef's Note

Allow the coated apples to sit for about 10 minutes before baking. This allows the apples time to absorb the spices and lemon juice, making for a tastier cobbler.

Apple Cobbler ✍

Yield: Makes one 13 by 9 1/2-inch deep-dish cobbler

Prep Time: 30 to 40 minutes

Crust Chill Time: 60 minutes

Total Time: 90 minutes

✍ Ingredients

Cobbler Crust

4 cups all-purpose flour

2 tablespoons granulated sugar

1 teaspoon salt

1 cup lard

1 cup (2 sticks) salted butter

1 egg

1 tablespoon distilled white vinegar

1/2 cup water

Apple Filling

2 tablespoons salted butter (to prepare baking dish)

7 or 8 large Golden Delicious or your favorite apples, peeled and cut into small slices

2/3 cup granulated sugar

2/3 cup brown sugar

1 1/2 teaspoons cinnamon

1/2 teaspoon ground nutmeg

2 tablespoons freshly squeezed lemon juice

2 tablespoons vanilla extract

1/2 cup (1 stick) salted butter, melted

1/2 teaspoon salt

Directions for Cobbler Crust

This recipe makes enough dough for two cobblers, so feel free to save the rest for later (or for another cobbler or pie).

1. Mix the flour, sugar, and salt, then add the lard and butter by cutting it into the mix. Set aside.

2. In a separate bowl beat the egg, then add the vinegar and water. Pour this mixture into the flour mixture and blend lightly.

3. Form the mixture into 2 balls and place in the refrigerator to chill for 30 to 45 minutes.

4. Remove 1 ball from the refrigerator. Roll out the dough into a 7-inch round, about 1/2 inch thick. Chill dough in the refrigerator as you prepare the apple filling.

Directions for Apple Filling

1. Preheat oven to 350°F. Butter the baking dish.

2. In a large bowl, mix the apples, sugars, cinnamon, freshly squeezed lemon juice, vanilla extract, butter, and salt together until well combined.

3. Toss apples well to coat evenly and turn into the prepared baking dish. Pinch off pieces of cobbler dough, flattening them into tiny pieces in your hand, and push them down into the apple filling. Some small pieces can be on the top, but most of these will be down inside the cobbler with the apples.

4. Bake cobbler at 350°F for 50 to 55 minutes until bubbly and crust is golden.

Serve hot with liberal helpings of old-fashioned vanilla ice cream.

Amazing!

My search for the greatest peaches in the world found me on the border of South Carolina and Georgia. Any sweet, ripe peach will work in this recipe, but for that rare period in summer when peaches are fresh and plentiful, this cobbler will reach deep into your soul.

You'll notice that the texture of the dough is formed just by pressing together the flat pieces of pastry, which bake thoroughly. This hot and bubbly masterpiece will be a dessert you'll always remember, so start peeling those peaches!

If you're ever fortunate enough to drive by a roadside peach stand in the summer, prepare to pull in and buy the freshest fruit nature has to offer. It's worth performing a U-turn to come back for this rare pleasure.

Chef's Note
Since peaches get sweeter and juicier as they ripen, squeezing them will tell you how ripe they are. Gently press or squeeze the shoulder and tip (where the stem was). If it just starts to give, it's ripe and ready.

Peach Cobbler ✌

Yield: Makes one
13 by 9 1/2-inch
deep-dish cobbler

Prep Time: 20 to 30 minutes

Crust Chill Time: 60 minutes

Total Time: 90 minutes

🥄 Ingredients

Cobbler Crust

4 cups all-purpose flour

2 tablespoons
granulated sugar

1 teaspoon salt

1 cup lard

1 cup (2 sticks) salted butter

1 egg

1 tablespoon distilled
white vinegar

1/2 cup water

Peach Filling

2 tablespoons salted butter
(to prepare baking dish)

7 or 8 large peaches,
peeled and sliced
into small pieces

1 cup granulated sugar

1 cup brown sugar

1 1/2 teaspoons cinnamon

1/2 teaspoon nutmeg

1/8 teaspoon allspice

1 teaspoon cornstarch

2 tablespoons freshly
squeezed lemon juice

2 tablespoons vanilla extract

1/2 cup (1 stick) salted butter,
melted

1/2 teaspoon salt

Directions for Cobbler Crust

This recipe makes enough dough for two cobblers, so feel free to save the rest for later (or for another cobbler or pie).

1. Mix the flour, sugar, and salt, then add the lard and butter by cutting it into the mix. Set aside.

2. In a separate bowl beat the egg, then add the vinegar and water. Pour this mixture into the flour mixture and lightly combine.

3. Form the mixture into 2 balls and place in the refrigerator to chill for 30 to 45 minutes.

4. Remove 1 ball from the refrigerator. Roll out the dough into a 7-inch round, about 1/2 inch thick. Chill dough in the refrigerator as you prepare the peach filling.

Directions for Peach Filling

1. Preheat oven to 350°F. Butter the baking dish.

2. In a large bowl, mix the sliced peaches, sugars, cinnamon, nutmeg, allspice, cornstarch, freshly squeezed lemon juice, vanilla extract, butter, and salt together until well blended.

3. Toss peaches to coat evenly, then pour filling into the prepared baking dish. Pinch off pieces of dough, flattening them into tiny pieces in your hand, and push them down into the filling. Add these dough pieces liberally.

4. Bake cobbler at 350°F for 50 to 55 minutes until bubbling and dough is golden.

Serve immediately with liberal helpings of French vanilla or your favorite vanilla ice cream.

Little Italy Cream Cake
(page 143)

There are several recipes for carrot cake, and some are noteworthy. But why not bake a carrot cake that will bring tears to your eyes? This is the one.

You'll notice that it has fresh carrots and pineapple with just the right amount of nuts and a moist texture that balances on your palate delightfully.

A frosting of lemon cream cheese adds the perfect complement, and it's okay to tell yourself it's healthy as you have a second slice. Remember: No one is watching.

Chef's Note

It's easy to make a great carrot cake cream cheese frosting. Just follow these two tricks:

First, start with cream cheese that is room temperature and butter that is soft but slightly firm and still holds its cube shape.

Next: Beat the room-temperature cream cheese well before adding the softened butter.

Carrot Cake ❧

Yield: Makes one 9-inch 3-layer cake

Prep Time: 30 minutes

Total Time: 90 minutes
Allow the cake to rest for 24 hours before serving.

🍴 Ingredients

Carrot Cake

3 cups corn oil

2 cups brown sugar, packed

2 cups granulated sugar

8 eggs

2 cups all-purpose flour

2 cups less 4 tablespoons whole wheat flour

2 teaspoons salt

4 teaspoons baking soda

4 teaspoons baking powder

4 teaspoons ground cinnamon

6 cups raw carrots, finely shredded and packed

1 pound (16 ounces) pineapple, crushed and drained

2 cups small pecan or walnut pieces, lightly toasted

Directions for Carrot Cake

Unfrosted, the cake may be wrapped in airtight plastic wrap and refrigerated for 5 to 6 days or frozen for 2 to 3 months. If frosted, the cake may be stored in the refrigerator for one week or more.

1. Preheat oven to 350°F.

2. Butter and lightly flour three 9-inch round cake pans.

3. In a large bowl, blend together the corn oil and sugars. Then add the eggs one at a time, beating until blended.

4. In another bowl, sift together flours, salt, baking soda, baking powder, and cinnamon.

5. Add the flour mixture about 1/3 cup at a time to the corn oil mixture, beating just enough to blend.

6. Fold the carrots into the mixture, followed by the pineapple. Add toasted nuts of your choice.

7. Pour the batter into three 9-inch round cake pans.

8. Bake at 350°F for 40 to 55 minutes or until a toothpick inserted in the center of each cake comes out barely moist or almost clean.

Cool the cakes in the pans on a rack for 10 minutes, then remove from pans, inverting onto wire rack to cool completely as you prepare the Lemon Cream Cheese Frosting (page 81).

Lemon Cream Cheese Frosting

Directions for Lemon Cream Cheese Frosting

1. In a large mixing bowl, mash the cream cheese. Add the softened butter, then mix together until well blended and creamy in texture.

2. Add the salt, vanilla extract, and freshly squeezed lemon juice to the mixture. Mix well.

3. Slowly add the confectioners' sugar and mix until well combined, taking care not to whip the frosting too much.

4. Add the fresh lemon zest, blending well.

Frost your cooled cake!

Yield: Makes frosting for one 9-inch cake

Prep Time: 15 minutes

Total Time: 30 minutes

Ingredients

Lemon Cream Cheese Frosting

16 ounces cream cheese (2 8-ounce packages), softened

1 cup (2 sticks) salted butter, softened

1/2 teaspoon salt

2 tablespoons vanilla extract

3 tablespoons freshly squeezed lemon juice

2 cups confectioners' sugar, sifted

2 tablespoons freshly grated lemon zest

Chef's Note

Refrigerate the frosting until 10 minutes before using. It's then the perfect consistency to hold its shape while piping.

❧ Grandma's Cake with Hot Bourbon Sauce

This cake is dazzling. Once you taste this recipe you'll probably say, "Where has it been all my life?"

Grandma's Cake with a complement of hot Bourbon Sauce is a flavorful reminder of grandmothers everywhere. This recipe honors the talented bakers of generations and may become a family tradition with you.

Tell grandma I said, "Hi."

Chef's Note

When you cook with bourbon or any other liquor, the harshness of the alcohol goes up with the steam and leaves a delicious flavor.

Grandma's Cake with Hot Bourbon Sauce ⤳

Yield: Makes one 8 by 8-inch
or 9 by 9-inch cake

Prep Time: 20 minutes

Total Time: 75 minutes

🥄 Ingredients

Grandma's Cake

2 cups flour

1 1/2 teaspoons baking soda

1/4 teaspoon salt

1 teaspoon cinnamon

1 teaspoon nutmeg

1 teaspoon allspice

1 cup vegetable oil

2 tablespoons salted butter,
melted

3 eggs, beaten

1 cup cultured buttermilk

1 1/2 cups granulated sugar

1 teaspoon vanilla extract

1 cup cooked prunes,
chopped and
mashed down

1 cup pecans or walnuts,
chopped

Directions for Grandma's Cake

1. Preheat oven to 325°F.

2. Butter and line an 8 by 8-inch or 9 by 9-inch baking pan with parchment paper.

3. Sift together the dry ingredients of flour, baking soda, salt, cinnamon, nutmeg, and allspice.

4. Combine vegetable oil, melted butter, eggs, cultured buttermilk, sugar, and vanilla extract into a mixing bowl and beat well.

5. Add the flour mixture to the batter 1/2 cup at a time, blending well with each addition.

6. Fold in the prunes and nuts.

7. Pour into prepared baking pan and bake for 45 to 55 minutes or until the center springs back when you touch it.

Remove from oven and let cake cool in pan for 10 minutes.

While cake is baking, prepare the Hot Bourbon Sauce (page 85).

🐦 Hot Bourbon Sauce

Directions for Hot Bourbon Sauce

1. In a small saucepan, mix the sugar, salt, cultured buttermilk (with dissolved baking soda), corn syrup, bourbon, butter, and vanilla extract and bring to a boil.

2. Cook for 1 minute, then set aside. Sauce is now ready to use.

Directions for Serving Grandma's Cake

1. Invert still-warm cake onto a serving platter.

2. Spoon with hot bourbon sauce and let it soak in, using all of the sauce.

3. Dust with confectioners' sugar.

Serve warm...and get outta the way!

Yield: Makes 4 cups of sauce
Prep Time: 5 minutes
Total Time: 15 minutes

Ingredients

Hot Bourbon Sauce

1 cup sugar

Pinch of salt

1/2 cup cultured buttermilk

1/2 teaspoon baking soda, dissolved in the buttermilk

1 tablespoon light corn syrup

1 tablespoon bourbon

6 tablespoons (3/4 stick) salted butter

1 teaspoon vanilla extract

1 tablespoon confectioners' sugar

Chef's Note

If your dessert doesn't look perfect, don't worry. It will still taste the same.

✂ Rick's Red Velvet Cake

I searched for years to find the perfect red velvet cake recipe, and I found it just outside of Orlando, Florida. The man who gave me the basics for this recipe made me swear I would never give it to anyone.

I lied.

The effect of this particular red velvet cake recipe is interesting. I served it to Barbra Streisand several years ago at a holiday party, and after she took one bite, she said, "Who did this? Who did this?"

I sheepishly raised my hand at the table and said, "I baked it."

She said, "No, you didn't."

I said, "No, I did."

And she said, "I have to have the recipe—give it to me."

When I told her that the man in Orlando made me promise to never give up the recipe, she slapped me…and I gave her the recipe.

Barbara has it now, and so do you. It's as smooth and rich as that beautiful voice of hers.

Rick's Red Velvet Cake ❧

Yield: Makes one 10-inch 3-layer cake

Prep Time: 25 minutes

Total Time: 90 minutes

🥄 Ingredients

Rick's Red Velvet Cake

3 tablespoons unsweetened cocoa powder for preparing cake pans

3 3/4 cups self-rising flour

2 1/4 cups granulated sugar

1 1/2 teaspoons baking soda

1 1/2 teaspoons unsweetened cocoa powder

1 teaspoon salt

3 large eggs, beaten

2 tablespoons vanilla extract

1 1/2 teaspoons distilled white vinegar

2/3 cup salted butter, softened

1 1/2 cups cultured buttermilk

2 cups vegetable oil

3 ounces red food coloring

👨‍🍳 Chef's Note

Mixing the cocoa powder and red food coloring together to form a paste helps evenly disperse the red food coloring when it is mixed into the batter. If the mixture is lumpy, a red spatula works best in bringing the mixture together (the red food coloring can stain light-colored spatulas).

Directions for Rick's Red Velvet Cake

Baking at a low temperature ensures the vegetable oil in the cake doesn't burn, so be sure to keep an eye on the oven temperature.

1. Preheat oven to 325°F.

2. Butter three 10-inch round cake pans. Line pan bottoms with parchment paper; butter the parchment. Sprinkle each pan with 1 tablespoon sifted cocoa powder, tapping pans to coat and discarding extra cocoa.

3. Sift together the dry ingredients of flour, sugar, baking soda, 1 1/2 teaspoons cocoa, and salt.

4. Mix together the wet ingredients of eggs, vanilla extract, vinegar, softened butter, cultured buttermilk, vegetable oil, and red food coloring.

5. Using a mixer, combine the wet ingredients with the dry ingredients until thoroughly blended, but not overly to the point of adding too much air to the batter.

6. Fill the 3 prepared 10-inch pans halfway with cake batter, leaving room for the cake to rise.

7. Bake for 45 to 60 minutes until inserted toothpick comes out clean. Take care not to overbake.

8. Remove the cakes from the oven, cool 15 minutes, then run a knife around the edges to loosen them from the baking pans. Invert the cakes onto a plate and then re-invert them onto a cooling rack. Let cool completely, then frost with White Chocolate Cream Cheese Frosting (page 89).

White Chocolate Cream Cheese Frosting

Directions for White Chocolate Cream Cheese Frosting

1. Using a handheld or stand mixer, beat together the butter and cream cheese until well incorporated and fluffy.

2. Place the white chocolate in the microwave for 30 seconds. Stir, then heat once more in microwave for another 30 seconds. Stir until smooth.

3. Add the melted white chocolate and salt to the cream cheese mixture, beating until smooth.

4. While mixing, slowly add confectioners' sugar, a little at a time.

5. Add vanilla extract, then the heavy cream, depending on what consistency you prefer.

6. Add chopped pecans and mix well.

Directions for Assembling Rick's Red Velvet Cake

1. Place first layer in the middle of cake stand. With a spatula spread some of the white chocolate cream cheese frosting over the top of the cake, spreading enough frosting to make a 1/4 to 1/2-inch layer.

2. Carefully set another layer on top and repeat. Top with the remaining layer and cover the entire cake with the remaining frosting.

3. Decorate with red velvet cake crumbs or chopped pecans.

Share immediately!

Yield: Makes frosting for one 10-inch cake

Prep Time: 25 minutes

Total Time: 90 minutes

Ingredients

White Chocolate Cream Cheese Frosting

1/2 cup (1 stick) salted butter, room temperature

1 8-ounce package of cream cheese, softened

4 ounces white chocolate (2/3 cup if using chocolate chips), melted

1/4 teaspoon salt

3 cups confectioners' sugar, sifted

1 tablespoon vanilla extract

1 to 2 tablespoons heavy cream

1 1/2 cups pecans, chopped

Chef's Note

Decorating tip: Use a round metal sieve (like you use to strain liquids) to make red velvet cake crumbs.

Cut a small piece of cake from top of the layer to level it. Rub cake piece against the bottom of the metal sieve, collecting the crumbs in a dish or bowl.

Use crumbs to decorate the sides and top edges of the cake after applying the frosting.

❧ Classic Chocolate Cake

Do you remember as a kid the tiny wisps of aroma extending from your kitchen as your mother or grandmother made the most delicious chocolate cake? I don't either.

That's why I went on a worldwide search to find the most delicious, moist, and ultimate "let's have another piece" rich chocolate cake.

The cake that wins the award is a chocolate cake inspired by Barbara Lowe from Westfield, North Carolina, a lovely lady with the most positive attitude I have ever experienced. She's the mom we all wish for, and her love for others manifests itself in her baking.

Barbara took two "starving students" under her wing years ago and shared the secret baking talents she had learned from "Mama Lowe." This cake recipe has been closely guarded until now.

No one minds if you slice it while it's still slightly warm and marry it to a large scoop of your favorite ice cream.
Go ahead: Put a candle on it—even if it's not your birthday.

Classic Chocolate Cake ❧

Yield: Makes one 9-inch 3-layer cake

Prep Time: 1 hour

Total Time: 3 hours (includes frosting chill time)

🥄 Ingredients

Classic Chocolate Cake

To Prepare Pans:

2 tablespoons butter

3 to 5 tablespoons unsweetened cocoa powder

For Cake:

1/2 cup unsweetened cocoa powder

1 cup warm water, divided

1/2 cup cultured buttermilk

1 1/2 cups cake flour

3/4 teaspoon baking soda

1/8 teaspoon salt

1/2 cup (1 stick) salted butter, room temperature

1 cup granulated sugar

1/2 cup brown sugar, packed

2 large eggs at room temperature, beaten

1 1/2 tablespoons vanilla extract

👨‍🍳 Chef's Note

Dusting your pans with cocoa powder instead of flour prevents the cake from sticking to the pan (just like flour does) while adding additional chocolate flavor.

Directions for Classic Chocolate Cake

1. Preheat oven to 350°F.

2. Butter three 9-inch cake pans with tall sides (about 1 1/2 inches high). Line bottom of pan with parchment paper. Butter both the pan and parchment paper. Dust with cocoa powder, discarding excess.

3. In a small bowl, whisk 1/2 cup cocoa powder with 1/2 cup warm water.

4. In a separate small bowl, whisk cultured buttermilk and remaining 1/2 cup of water.

5. Sift cake flour, baking soda, and salt in a medium-sized bowl.

6. In a large mixing bowl, cream the butter and sugars for about 5 minutes until the batter becomes pale yellow and fluffy. It will gain a bit in volume and be somewhat granular.

7. Gradually add beaten eggs, then beat until smooth and fluffy, about 1 minute.

8. Add cocoa mixture and beat well.

9. While mixing, add the flour mixture in 3 additions, alternating with the buttermilk mixture. Add vanilla extract.

10. Divide the batter evenly between the three 9-inch cake pans.

11. Bake at 350°F for 18 minutes or until a toothpick inserted into the center comes out clean. Remove from oven and allow the layers to cool in the cake pans on a wire rack.

12. When ready to frost cake: Run a knife gently around the edges of the cake pan to loosen. Cover cake pan with a plate, then quickly invert. Remove the parchment paper.

Transfer to cake stand and frost with Chocolate Frosting (page 93).

🌿 Chocolate Frosting

Directions for Chocolate Frosting

1. In a medium-sized bowl, combine sugar, cocoa, espresso powder, and salt. Blend well with fork or wire whisk.

2. Melt butter in a medium-sized saucepan over medium heat. Add the cocoa mixture, stirring until thoroughly combined.

3. Gradually add the heavy cream, stirring constantly.

4. Stir until the chocolate mixture becomes very hot and just begins to simmer along the edges of the saucepan.

5. Reduce heat to low, stirring mixture for about 1 more minute. The frosting will look like chocolate sauce (and taste that yummy, too!).

6. Remove from heat. Transfer mixture to a medium-sized bowl, add vanilla extract and stir.

7. Chill frosting until just thickened—about 1 1/2 hours, stirring occasionally.

8. When ready for use, remove frosting from refrigerator. Spread onto cake when frosting is room temperature.

9. Cut into slices and serve.

Be forewarned: This one will go fast!

Yield: Makes frosting for one 9-inch cake

Prep Time: 15 minutes

Chill Time: 1 1/2 hours

Total Time: Approximately 2 hours

Ingredients 🥄

Chocolate Frosting

1 1/3 cups brown sugar, packed

1 cup unsweetened cocoa powder

2 teaspoons espresso powder

1/4 teaspoon salt

10 tablespoons (1 1/4 sticks) unsalted butter

1 cup heavy cream

1 1/2 tablespoons vanilla extract

✌ Lemon Drizzle Cake

What would happen if you baked the perfect pound cake with a unique flavor and consistency you've never before experienced, then drizzled a fresh and sweet lemon concoction on top? You would be trapped under the spell of Lemon Drizzle Cake.

Use fresh lemons and allow the syrup to ooze down inside the cake from tiny slits in the golden top. It's amazing how moist this cake stays for several days.

It's quick to make, fast to bake…so bake it now, for Heaven's sake.

Chef's Note
Use a skewer to poke holes into the cake before adding the glaze. This will help the cake absorb more of the glaze's lemony flavor.

Lemon Drizzle Cake ❧

Yield: Makes one 9-inch cake

Prep Time: 15 minutes

Total Time: 60 minutes

🥄 Ingredients

Lemon Drizzle Cake

1 1/2 cups all-purpose flour

2 teaspoons baking powder

1/2 teaspoon salt

3 large eggs

1 cup sour cream

1 cup granulated sugar

1 tablespoon vanilla extract

2 tablespoons grated lemon zest

2/3 cup vegetable oil

3 tablespoons salted butter, melted

Lemon Sugar Glaze

3/4 cup granulated sugar

1/3 cup freshly squeezed lemon juice

1 teaspoon vanilla extract

Vanilla Drizzle

1 1/2 cups confectioners' sugar, sifted to remove lumps

2 tablespoons freshly squeezed lemon juice

Pinch of salt (1/8 teaspoon)

1 to 2 tablespoons cultured buttermilk

Directions for Lemon Drizzle Cake

1. Preheat oven to 350°F. No mixer is needed to make this cake!

2. Butter and lightly flour a 9-inch Bundt™ pan.

3. Sift together the flour, baking powder, and salt.

4. In another bowl, whisk together the eggs, sour cream, sugar, vanilla extract, and lemon zest.

5. Slowly whisk the flour mixture into the liquid mixture. With a rubber spatula, fold the vegetable oil and butter into the batter, making sure it is incorporated.

6. Pour the batter into the prepared pan and bake at 350°F for about 40 to 50 minutes or until a long toothpick inserted in the middle comes out clean.

Directions for Lemon Sugar Glaze

1. While cake is baking, cook the sugar and lemon juice in a small pan until the sugar dissolves and the mixture is clear. Remove from heat and add 1 teaspoon vanilla extract. Set aside.

2. Allow cake to cool for 10 minutes in the pan after removing from oven, then invert it onto serving plate.

3. While cake is still warm, spoon the lemon sugar glaze over the cake, allowing glaze to soak in the cake as it cools—about 15 minutes.

Directions for Vanilla Drizzle

Sift confectioners' sugar in a medium-sized bowl. Slowly stir in the freshly squeezed lemon juice a little at a time. Add salt, and enough buttermilk to make a smooth, pourable drizzle.

Spoon all over top of cake in a zigzag pattern.

Mmmmmmmmmmm-arvelous!

◥ Classic White Coconut Cake

When it comes to sheer eye appeal, this Classic White Coconut Cake leads the pack. Under a glass dome, it becomes the centerpiece of any kitchen or dining room table. Fresh coconut is not required, but I like to mash the coconut into the frosting by hand. It gives it a homemade look, and on a few slices somebody gets a little more coconut and a lot more smiles.

Classic White Coconut Cake ๛

Yield: Makes one 10-inch 3-layer cake

Prep Time: 45 minutes

Total Time: 60 minutes

🥄 Ingredients

Classic White Coconut Cake

2 sticks (1 cup) salted butter, room temperature

2 cups granulated sugar

4 eggs

3 cups self-rising flour, sifted

1 cup coconut milk

3 teaspoons vanilla extract

Coconut Cream Filling

3/4 cup granulated sugar

1 cup sour cream

4 tablespoons milk

1/2 cup flaked, sweetened coconut

👨‍🍳 Chef's Note

Room temperature ingredients will make all the difference with this cake. Unchilled egg whites will give you super-tall, ultra-lightly beaten egg whites.

Directions for Classic White Coconut Cake

1. Preheat oven to 350°F.

2. Butter and lightly flour three 10-inch cake pans.

3. Beat butter until creamy and fluffy in texture. Add sugar and continue to cream well for 3 to 5 minutes.

4. Add the eggs one at a time, beating well after each addition.

5. Add the flour and coconut milk alternately to creamed mixture, beginning and ending the process with flour.

6. Add the vanilla extract and continue to beat until just mixed.

7. Divide the batter equally among the 3 prepared 10-inch cake pans. Level the batter in each pan by holding the pans 3 to 4 inches above the counter, then dropping flat onto the counter. Do this several times to release any air bubbles and assure you of a more level cake.

8. Bake at 350°F for 25 to 30 minutes. Allow to cool in the pans for 5 to 10 minutes. Invert cakes onto cooling racks and set aside.

Directions for Coconut Cream Filling

In a bowl, stir together the sugar, sour cream, milk, and coconut until well blended. Set aside.

✑ Seven-Minute White Frosting

Directions for Seven-Minute White Frosting

1. Place the sugar, cream of tartar, corn syrup, salt, water, and egg whites into the top pan of a double boiler. Beat with a handheld electric mixer for 1 minute.

2. Place the pan over boiling water, being sure that the boiling water does not touch the bottom of the top pan. Beat constantly on high speed with a handheld electric mixer for 7 minutes, or until the frosting will stand in soft peaks.

3. Beat in the vanilla extract and set aside.

Directions for Assembling Classic White Coconut Cake

1. Put the first cake layer onto a pedestal. Using a meat fork, poke holes approximately 1 inch apart until the entire cake has been evenly poked.

2. Spread a third of the coconut cream filling on top of the bottom cake layer up to the edges. Top with the second cake layer, making sure that the layers are leveled, and repeat poking and coconut-filling-spreading process.

3. As each layer is stacked, stick them with toothpicks to prevent cake from shifting. Top with the last cake layer.

4. Frost the top and sides of the cake with the Seven-Minute white frosting. Garnish with flaked coconut, sprinkling on top and pressing into sides of the cake.

Yield: Makes frosting for one 10-inch cake

Prep Time: 5 minutes

Total Time: 15 minutes

Ingredients 🥄

Seven-Minute White Frosting

1 1/2 cups granulated sugar

1/4 teaspoon cream of tartar

1 tablespoon light corn syrup

1/4 teaspoon salt

1/3 cup water

4 egg whites

1 1/2 teaspoons vanilla extract

2 to 3 cups coconut, flaked and sweetened

Quick Coconut Cake ᰍ

Yield: Makes one 8-inch
3-layer cake

Prep Time: 45 minutes

Total Time: 60 minutes

🥄 Ingredients

Quick Coconut Cake

2 boxes white cake mix
(Betty Crocker® Super Moist
White Cake Mix suggested)

2 cups coconut milk

2/3 cup vegetable oil

6 eggs

Coconut Buttercream
Frosting

2 cups (4 sticks) salted butter,
softened

4 tablespoons vanilla extract

1/2 teaspoon salt

4 cups confectioners' sugar,
sifted

4 tablespoons half & half

2 to 3 cups coconut,
flaked and sweetened

👨‍🍳 Chef's Note

Double-line your cake pans
with parchment paper.
This helps reduce the
chances of overbaking
and keeps your cake moist.

When you don't have enough time for the traditional coconut cake, here's a quick alternative using white cake mix and quick buttercream frosting.

Directions for Quick Coconut Cake

1. Heat oven to 350°F (325°F for dark or nonstick pans).

2. Grease three 8-inch baking pans with shortening or cooking spray; line with parchment paper.

3. Make white cake mix as directed on box, substituting coconut milk for water. Add oil and eggs. Beat for 2 minutes, then pour batter into prepared baking pans.

4. Bake 30 to 35 minutes or until toothpick inserted in center comes out clean. Cool completely in pan on cooling rack, at least 1 hour.

Directions for Coconut Buttercream Frosting

1. In a bowl, cream the softened butter and vanilla extract. Add salt and blend well.

2. Add confectioners' sugar 1/2 cup at a time, alternating with tablespoons of half & half until light and fluffy.

3. Spread onto top of cake and around the sides.

4. Decorate with flaked coconut, pressing it into the top and sides. Lightly toasting the coconut is optional.

✎ Cola Cake

Whoever thought the secret to a moist, rich, chocolaty cake would be the addition of good ol' cola?

Well, it just so happens that adding your favorite cola (you know which one) to this cake recipe imparts a flavor that you and your guests will savor for some time to come.

The frosting marries to the cake, and together they both taste like they're on a honeymoon.

Enjoy this cola cake and as always, follow me and add a generous dollop of the ice cream of your choice.

Chef's Note

If you dare, use mayonnaise instead of cultured buttermilk. You'll get a moister, creamier chocolate cake.

Cola Cake ❧

Yield: Makes one
9 by13-inch cake
Prep Time: 20 minutes
Total Time: 25 to 35 minutes

🥄 Ingredients

Cola Cake

1 cup Coca-Cola®
2/3 cup corn oil
1/2 cup vegetable oil
1/2 cup (1 stick) salted butter
2 heaping tablespoons
dark cocoa powder
2 heaping tablespoons
regular cocoa powder
2 cups granulated sugar
2 cups all-purpose flour
1/2 teaspoon salt
2 large eggs
1/2 cup cultured buttermilk
1 teaspoon baking soda
2 tablespoons
vanilla extract

Cola Cake
Chocolate Frosting

1/2 cup (1 stick) salted butter
2 tablespoons dark
cocoa powder
1 tablespoon regular
cocoa powder
6 tablespoons half & half
2 tablespoons vanilla extract
1/2 teaspoon salt
4 1/2 cups
confectioners' sugar,
sifted

Directions for Cola Cake

1. Preheat oven to 350°F.

2. Butter and lightly flour a 9 by 13-inch sheet cake pan.

3. In a saucepan combine Coca-Cola®, corn oil, vegetable oil, butter, and both cocoas. Bring to a boil.

4. In a separate bowl, mix together the sugar, flour, and salt.

5. Pour the boiling Coca-Cola® mixture into the flour mixture and beat until well blended. Add the eggs, cultured buttermilk, baking soda, and vanilla extract to the batter and beat well.

6. Pour the batter into the prepared 9 by 13-inch sheet cake pan.

7. Bake at 350°F for 30 minutes or until a toothpick inserted into the center comes out almost clean.

Directions for Cola Cake Chocolate Frosting

1. Combine the butter and cocoas in a saucepan and heat the mixture until it melts. Add the half & half. Stir until well blended.

2. Beat in the vanilla extract, salt, and confectioners' sugar.

3. Spread the frosting onto the hot cake while it is still warm. Cool and cut, serving with a dollop of your favorite vanilla ice cream.

Mmmmmmmmmmm!

Chef's Note

Use shiny pans to bake your chocolate cake.
Dark pans cause the edges to darken and toughen.

Cinnamon Coffee Cake

They say that breakfast is the most important meal of the day. If this is true, then the most important dessert of the morning is cinnamon coffee cake.

Share the fabulous essence of fresh cinnamon as it permeates your entire abode. A cup of coffee, warm cinnamon coffee cake, and checking your device in solitude is what starting the day is all about.

You'll be pleasantly surprised at how quickly you assemble these savory and succulent ingredients. Start your day the right way—with freshly baked cinnamon coffee cake.

Cinnamon Coffee Cake 〜

Yield: Makes one 8 by 4-inch cake

Prep Time: 20 minutes

Total Time: 60 minutes

 Ingredients

Cinnamon Coffee Cake

1 cup granulated sugar

1/2 cup (1 stick) salted butter

1 large egg

1 tablespoon vanilla extract

1 1/2 cups all-purpose flour

3 teaspoons baking powder

1/2 teaspoon salt

1/2 cup half & half

Cinnamon Crumble

1/2 cup brown sugar

2 tablespoons flour

3 teaspoons cinnamon

4 tablespoons salted butter, melted

Chef's Note

Mixing this recipe by hand avoids one of the biggest risks: overmixing. The less you mix, the lighter this cake will be.

To test for doneness, stick a toothpick into the center of the cake—it should come out with just a few crumbs attached.

Directions for Cinnamon Coffee Cake

1. Preheat oven to 350°F.

2. Butter an 8 by 4-inch baking pan and line the bottom with parchment paper. Butter the parchment paper and dust with flour.

3. Combine the sugar and butter and beat until smooth.

4. Add the egg and vanilla extract and blend well.

5. Toss together the remaining dry ingredients of flour, baking powder, and salt in a bowl.

6. Add the flour mixture to the batter, alternating with half & half, mixing well.

Directions for Cinnamon Crumble

1. Pour half the batter into the prepared 8 by 4-inch baking pan.

2. In a medium-sized bowl mix together brown sugar, flour, and cinnamon. Add melted butter and mix until crumbly.

3. Sprinkle the batter with half of the cinnamon mixture. Add second half of batter, then add the remaining cinnamon mixture on top.

4. Bake at 375°F for 40 to 50 minutes or until a long toothpick inserted in the center comes out almost clean.

Serve warm.

Fabulous!

Don't tell Mama how easy this cake is to bake!

The history of this cake goes all the way back to the Spanish explorers who discovered America off the coast of the Florida peninsula. The sugar cane fields in that region yielded some of the finest-quality sugar in the world.

From this starting point, the sugar was browned and prepared for the cake. The sumptuous drippings that crown the rich, moist cake make it a luxurious and splendid ending to any meal.

Don't tell Mama…because she'll want an extra piece, and you know she likes to watch her waistline. A side dish of ice cream is recommended.

Have fun—and watch how easy this one is to bake.

Chef's Note
Garnish the top with confectioners' sugar and toasted coconut for a special touch.

Don't Tell Mama Cake ❧

Yield: Makes one 9-inch Bundt™ cake

Prep Time: 25 minutes

Total Time: 60 minutes

 Ingredients

Don't Tell Mama Cake

2 eggs

2 cups granulated sugar

1/2 cup vegetable oil

2 heaping tablespoons unsweetened cocoa powder

1/2 cup cultured buttermilk

1 teaspoon baking soda

1 tablespoon vanilla extract

2 cups cake flour

1/4 teaspoon salt

1 cup water, boiling

Coconut Praline Topping

1/2 cup (1 stick) salted butter, melted

16 ounces light brown sugar

2 cups coconut, shredded and divided

3/4 to 1 cup chopped pecans

1 can (5 ounces) evaporated milk

2 tablespoons vanilla extract

1/4 teaspoon salt

Confectioners' sugar for garnish

👨‍🍳 Chef's Note

The cake gets more moist and delicious after sitting for 24 hours.

Directions for Don't Tell Mama Cake

1. Preheat oven to 350°F.

2. Butter and lightly flour a Bundt™ pan. Set aside.

3. Mix together the eggs, sugar, vegetable oil, cocoa, cultured buttermilk, baking soda, vanilla extract, cake flour, and salt, adding the boiling water last.

4. Pour the mixture into the prepared Bundt™ pan.

5. Bake at 350°F for 30 to 40 minutes or until an inserted toothpick comes out almost clean. Remove from oven and set aside.

Directions for Coconut Praline Topping

In a large saucepan, mix the butter, light brown sugar, 1 cup of coconut, pecans, evaporated milk, vanilla extract, and salt over medium heat, stirring well and constantly until bubbly. Remove from heat.

Directions for Assembling Don't Tell Mama Cake

1. Remove the cake from the Bundt™ pan and invert onto cake stand or plate.

2. Pour the warm coconut praline topping into the center hole of the cake.

3. Let the cake stand for a while to set up and not ooze too much.

4. Before serving, toast reserved 1 cup coconut in 350°F oven for 5 minutes. Sprinkle on top of warm coconut praline topping. Dust with confectioners' sugar.

Serve sliced, topped with a dollop of your favorite vanilla ice cream.

Heavenly!

❧ Molten Chocolate Cake

Let's bring a personal party to each person sitting at the table. With these individual molten chocolate cakes, every guest feels as if he or she is getting something special.

And they are!

Piercing the center of this cake allows the rich chocolate goo to ooze onto the plate, ready to be lapped up.
I hope your tongue is as long as mine.

Round up the ramekins and let's get the party started!

Molten Chocolate Cake ❧

Yield: Makes four 6-ounce individual cakes

Prep Time: 20 minutes

Total Time: 35 minutes

🍴 Ingredients

Molten Chocolate Cake

2 tablespoons salted butter (to prepare ramekins)

4 tablespoons unsweetened cocoa powder (to prepare ramekins)

2 eggs

2 egg yolks

1/4 cup granulated sugar

Pinch of salt

1/2 cup (1 stick) unsalted butter

8 ounces bittersweet chocolate

1 tablespoon vanilla extract

2 tablespoons all-purpose flour

Confectioners' sugar (for garnish)

👨‍🍳 Chef's Note

How do you know when the batter is ready for the chocolate? When the egg and sugar mixture quadruples in volume. It gets there faster when the eggs are at room temperature.

Directions for Molten Chocolate Cake

1. Preheat oven to 450°F.

2. Generously butter 4 ramekins. Lightly dust with 2 tablespoons cocoa powder, tapping out the excess. Set prepared ramekins on a baking sheet.

3. In a medium-sized bowl, beat the eggs, egg yolks, sugar, and salt at high speed until thickened and pale. Set aside.

4. In a double boiler over simmering water, melt 1/2 cup butter with 8 ounces of bittersweet chocolate. Add vanilla extract.

5. Whisk the chocolate until smooth. Fold it quickly into the egg mixture along with the 2 tablespoons of flour.

6. Spoon the batter into the prepared ramekins.

7. Bake at 400°F for 9 to 12 minutes or until the sides of the cakes are firm but the centers are soft.

8. Let the cakes cool in the ramekins for 1 minute, then cover each with an inverted dessert plate. Carefully turn each cake over; let stand for 10 seconds and then unmold.

9. Lightly dust with confectioners' sugar and serve immediately.

Delectable!

❧ Ruth's Pound Cake

There is a beautiful lady in Conway, South Carolina, who remembers the classic tradition of Southern pound cake. Her name is Ruth Wineglass—and yes, that's her real name.

Ruth told me personally, "Son, don't mess around with pound cake. It's called pound cake for a reason: a pound of eggs, a pound of butter, a pound of sugar, and so on."

If you just follow Ruth's simple instructions, the result will be a pound cake that is rich, moist, and full of flavor.

It's not necessary to have a topping, but if you must, I have included recipes for both the World's #1 Hot Fudge Sauce and an easy-to-make Caramel Sauce.

Get ready for Ruth's Pound Cake!

Chef's Note
Some chefs will want to invert this cake when serving, but you shouldn't. This cake is made to be sliced while warm with its buttery cracked top crust in full view.

Ruth's Pound Cake ❧

Yield: Makes one 9- or 10-inch tube cake

Prep Time: 20 minutes

Total Time: 2 hours

🥄 Ingredients

Prepare Tube Pan

2 tablespoons butter

1/2 cup flour

Ruth's Pound Cake

4 cups all-purpose flour, sifted twice

1/2 teaspoon salt

2 teaspoons baking powder

1/2 teaspoon baking soda

2 cups (4 sticks) salted butter, room temperature

3 1/2 cups sugar, comprised of 1 3/4 cups granulated sugar and 1 3/4 cups light brown sugar

5 whole eggs, room temperature

5 egg yolks, room temperature

1 cup cultured buttermilk

2 tablespoons vanilla extract

Confectioners' sugar (for garnish)

Prepare Ingredients and Tube Pan

1. Set out the butter and eggs, allowing them to come to room temperature.

2. Prepare a 9- or 10-inch tube pan: Butter well, then dust with flour. Set aside.

Directions for Ruth's Pound Cake

1. Sift flour. Add salt, baking powder, and baking soda to flour, then sift the mixture once more. Set aside.

2. Beat the butter until creamy and the mixture is smooth and light.

3. Add sugars, alternating the addition of granulated sugar and light brown sugar, creaming well as you add each addition.

4. Add the eggs one at a time, beating well after each addition.

5. Alternately add flour mixture and cultured buttermilk to batter, mixing well after each addition. Mix enough to incorporate, being careful not to overmix. Fold in vanilla extract last.

6. Pour batter into the prepared tube pan and put into a cold oven.

7. Bake at 300°F until a toothpick inserted into the center of the cake comes out clean—approximately 1 hour and 20 minutes.

Check for doneness after 1 hour, then in 10-minute increments thereafter. The top of the cake should be golden brown and slightly cracked. It's done when a toothpick inserted in the cake's center comes out clean.

After removing the cake from the oven, set on a wire rack and allow to cool for 10 minutes before removing from the tube pan.

We prefer to serve freshly sliced warm pound cake plain. For a more festive presentation, dust cake with confectioners' sugar before slicing.

For special occasions, drizzle cake with either the World's #1 Hot Fudge Sauce (page 179) or freshly made Caramel Sauce (page 217) before slicing.

Chef's Note

Ruth closely guarded these secrets to her taste sensation... but we'll share them with you:

1. Set the eggs and butter out for several hours in advance. They should both be room temperature. Adding cold eggs to warm butter will cause them to seize.

   Don't be tempted to cheat by softening butter in the microwave. It will get too hot—and partially melted butter doesn't perform properly in the creaming stage.

2. Sift the flour twice. This keeps it light, not dense, making for a fluffier texture. Add the baking powder, salt, and baking soda to the second sifting.

3. Take time to thoroughly cream the butter and sugars. Expect to use your stand or electric mixer for at least 5 minutes. The batter should be very pale in color.

4. Yes, you really do need to use butter for pound cake. The sharp edges of the sugar granules slice through butter, creating air pockets that expand further when baked. Only butter captures and holds these pockets, so there really is no substitute.

5. The biggest secret: Bake cake in a cold oven. You heard me. Don't preheat the oven. Put the cake batter into a cold oven and turn the temperature to 300°F. Set it, and forget it. Don't even open the door for the first hour...(you will be tempted because the aroma will be amazing!).

   Baking in a cold oven allows for more even cooking; it gives the baking powder time to produce more carbon dioxide bubbles. Plus, a cold oven contains more moisture than does its hot counterpart, yielding a nice, thick crust when the oven reacts to the starch in the batter. The result: a tall cake with a wonderful soft crumb inner texture, topped by a golden crisp sugary outer crust.

❧ Moravian "OMG" Cake

This ultra-rich, moist cake evolved in the mid-1700s. The Moravians, a group of Czech immigrants, experimented with several recipes and concluded that this cake, with its wonderful cinnamon and butter flavor, was enough to make them forget how much their wool underwear itched.

The buttery richness is created with yeast-raised bread dough that is characterized by small craters filled with brown sugar, butter, and cinnamon. Potatoes make the cake moist and supple, imparting a classic, homemade flavor.

Just out of the oven, the cake's golden topping is smooth, but left to cool for half an hour, it descends and produces the cake's characteristic dimpled appearance.

Moravian "OMG" Cake is a dessert that is easy and quick to assemble, and its deep, luscious flavor begs for a cup of home-brewed fresh coffee or tea. Indulge in a bite of this Old World Moravian cake and you'll be sure to exclaim, "OMG—it's *gooooood!*"

Chef's Note
While either potato buds or potato flakes work well, avoid potato granules, which can give the cake a different flavor.

Moravian "OMG" Cake ❧

Yield: Makes one 10 by 7-inch cake

Prep Time: 30 minutes

Total Time: 1 hour 30 minutes

🥄 Ingredients

Moravian "OMG" Cake

3/4 cup milk, heated to 110°F

1 1/2 teaspoons instant or rapid-rise yeast

1/3 cup granulated sugar

4 tablespoons salted butter, softened

1 large egg

1/4 cup instant Potato Buds™ or instant potato flakes (Optional: 1/2 cup plain mashed potatoes)

1/2 teaspoon salt

2 cups all-purpose flour, sifted

Brown Sugar Topping

6 tablespoons salted butter, cut into 1/2-inch pieces and chilled

1 1/2 cups packed light brown sugar

1 tablespoon ground cinnamon

Directions for Moravian "OMG" Cake

1. Adjust oven rack to middle position and heat to 200°F. Maintain temperature for 10 minutes and then turn off oven. This will properly prepare the oven for a low-level warmth needed for later steps.

2. Grease a medium-sized bowl and a 10 by 7-inch baking pan.

3. Stir warm milk and yeast together until yeast is fully dissolved. Cover with plastic wrap and let sit for about 15 minutes, allowing yeast to bubble in the warm milk.

4. Cream granulated sugar and softened butter. Add egg, potato buds, and salt.

5. With spatula, add yeast mixture to batter. Fold in flour until well blended.

6. Transfer dough to butter-prepared bowl. Cover with plastic and place in warm oven that is turned off. Let rise until doubled in size, about 30 minutes.

7. Remove from oven and press dough into prepared baking pan. Cover pan with plastic and again place in warm oven. Let rise until doubled in size, about 30 minutes.

8. Meanwhile, prepare topping by combining chilled butter, brown sugar, and cinnamon. Rub the butter pieces and brown sugar/cinnamon together with your fingers until the mix is like a coarse meal.

9. Remove pan from warm oven. Now the oven can be turned on and heated to 375°F. Indent surface of dough with thumbs and sprinkle with brown sugar mixture, pushing some down into the indentations in the dough.

10. Once oven is fully heated, bake until topping is bubbling and golden, 18 to 22 minutes. Let cool 30 minutes to allow cake's characteristic crevices to form. Serve.

Cooled cake can be wrapped with plastic and stored at room temperature for up to 2 days. But it probably won't last that long...

🌿 Chocolate Swirl Cheesecake

Several years ago in my secret test kitchen, I experimented with the flavors of chocolate and cheesecake. They quickly became fast friends.

With just the right amount of cream cheese and chocolate combined with the buttery crumbs of graham crackers, you'll love the results.

Swirling the chocolate for the design on the top is simple to do and gives it an artistic flair. As a centerpiece dessert, it stands up to any judge's critical eye.

Chocolate Swirl Cheesecake will be one of your favorites!

Chef's Note
Use a straight-edge knife to cut your cheesecake. Warm the blade in hot water, dry, and slice. Wipe clean and rewarm the knife after each cut.

Chocolate Swirl Cheesecake ❧

Yield: Makes one 9-inch cheesecake

Prep Time: 20 minutes

Chill Time: 3 to 4 hours

Total Time: 5 1/2 hours

🥄 Ingredients

Graham Cracker Crust

1 1/4 cups graham cracker crumbs

1/2 cup granulated sugar

1/2 cup (1 stick) salted butter, melted

1/8 teaspoon salt

Vanilla Cheesecake Filling

4 8-ounce packages (4 cups) of cream cheese, softened

1 1/2 cups granulated sugar

1 cup sour cream

2 tablespoons vanilla extract

8 eggs

Chocolate Cheesecake Filling

2 cups semisweet chocolate chips

1 cup granulated sugar

Directions for Graham Cracker Crust

NOTE: This makes enough graham cracker crust to line the bottom of a 9-inch springform baking pan. To prepare a crust that reaches up the sides of the cheesecake pan, double graham cracker crust portions.

1. Preheat oven to 375°F.

2. Mix the graham cracker crumbs, sugar, melted butter, and salt together until well incorporated.

3. Butter springform baking pan well along the bottom and sides.

4. Press graham cracker mixture into buttered pan.

5. Bake at 375°F for 10 minutes. Remove from oven and set aside to cool.

Directions for Cheesecake Filling

1. Preheat oven to 325°F.

2. In a large bowl, beat the cream cheese until creamy. Add sugar gradually, mixing well.

3. Add sour cream and vanilla extract. Next add the eggs, one at a time, beating after each addition.

4. Melt the chocolate chips in a microwavable bowl in microwave or over a slow double boiler until smooth. Stir in 1 cup of sugar and blend well.

5. Reserve about 1/4 of the vanilla batter in a medium-sized bowl for the chocolate mixture. Slowly mix the melted chocolate into the reserved vanilla batter, blending well.

6. Pour the chocolate cheesecake batter into the bottom of the prepared springform pan. Next pour the vanilla cheesecake batter on top of the chocolate batter layer.

   For a smaller 8-inch pan, fill to about 1/2 inch from the top of the springform pan.

7. Using a knife, swirl figure eights in the batter to give a marbled effect inside.

   TIP: To add decorative chocolate swirls to the top, reserve 2 to 4 cups of the chocolate batter. Carefully pour chocolate batter on top of vanilla batter in an inward spiral—winding around inside edge of springform pan in a consecutively smaller spiraling circle until reaching the center. Use a chopstick or straw and zigzag in and out (left to right, then repeat) through the chocolate stripe to create ribbon-like swirling effect.

8. Bake at 325°F for 50 minutes until a 2-inch circle in the middle is the only part that jiggles.

Remove from oven and allow to cool to room temperature. Refrigerate for 3 to 4 hours before serving to allow center to fully firm up.

Scrumptious!

Chef's Note

To get your cheesecake to its final firm, velvety texture is a 2-step process and takes some time.

First, allow the cake to cool to room temperature (about 2 hours); this prevents its top from cracking.

Afterwards, chill the cooled cheesecake in the refrigerator for 3 to 4 hours. This allows the interior of the cake to firm up so it is perfect for serving. Don't skip the chilling!

✌ Chocolate Red Robin

If you've ever been to New Orleans, you know that Cajuns take their desserts very seriously.

I am told that a requirement for high school graduation in The Big Easy is eating a pound of butter. The abundance of fine dining and luscious desserts is a one-of-a-kind delight. A New Orleans-trained chef who appreciates creative pastries is the world-famous chef Neil DeVries, who transplanted his skills to Hollywood, California.

Enter world-famous chef Neil DeVries.

Under threat of house arrest, he surrendered this recipe to me behind the clubhouse of the Lakeside Golf Club of Hollywood, California.

With the talented and lightly floured hands of pastry artist Yukie Fujimoto and inspired by the classic beignets of New Orleans, this ball of deliciousness explodes with flavor and will have your guests asking, "Who came up with this? Where did you find it?"

Your lips must remain sealed to protect Chef Neil.

Introducing Chocolate Red Robin...

Chocolate Red Robin

Yield: Makes 9 doughnuts

Prep Time: 20 minutes

Chill Time: 3 to 4 hours

Cooling Time: About 2 hours

Total Time: About 6 hours

 Ingredients

Red Robin Truffle Cake

8 ounces bittersweet chocolate, finely chopped

1 cup (2 sticks) unsalted butter, cut into 1-inch pieces

6 large eggs, room temperature

3/4 cup granulated sugar

1/4 cup all-purpose flour, sifted

2 tablespoons vanilla extract

Panko & Graham Cracker Coating Batter

Vegetable oil for deep-frying

2 large eggs

Pinch of salt

1 1/2 cups panko bread crumbs

1 cup all-purpose flour

1 1/2 cups graham cracker crumbs

Chef's Note

You can fry the doughnuts 2 to 4 hours ahead and reheat just before serving.

Directions for Red Robin Truffle Cake (for doughnuts)

1. Place the chocolate in a medium-sized heatproof bowl. Place the butter in a saucepan over medium heat. Place the bowl with the chocolate over the saucepan to warm the chocolate as the butter melts.

2. When the butter has melted, pour it over the chocolate. Stir until the chocolate has fully melted and has reached 100°F. Set aside in a warm place to keep the mixture hot.

3. In a large bowl, combine 6 eggs and sugar. Beat on medium speed until just lemony yellow and doubled in volume, about 3 minutes.

4. Whisk the flour into the chocolate mixture. Turn the mixer to low speed and add the hot chocolate batter to the eggs all at once. Scrape down the bowl and continue to mix until well combined.

5. Line an 8-inch square baking pan with parchment paper. Pour the chocolate truffle batter into the pan. Cover with plastic wrap and place in the freezer. Allow to freeze solid, at least 4 hours.

6. Lightly dust a work surface with flour. Remove frozen batter from freezer and run a knife around the edges of the pan, flipping the frozen batter over onto the work surface.

7. Peel off the parchment. Dust the batter lightly with flour, and using a 2 1/2-inch doughnut cutter dipped in flour, cut out 9 doughnuts. Place the doughnuts on a half-sheet pan, returning them to the freezer if not cooking right away.

8. Using a deep-fry thermometer, heat about 3 inches of vegetable oil to 350°F in a deep skillet, saucepan, or wok.

9. In a medium-sized bowl, whisk together the 2 eggs with the pinch of salt. Set aside. Place the panko bread crumbs in a medium-sized bowl, with the graham cracker crumbs in its own separate medium-sized bowl.

10. Spread 1 cup flour on a piece of parchment. One at a time, dust each doughnut generously with the flour, then dip into the eggs and tap off the excess. Place in the panko and coat evenly. Dip doughnut once more in the egg mixture, then into the graham cracker crumbs.

11. Using a slotted metal spoon, carefully place one doughnut at a time in the hot oil. Deep fry for 1 minute, then flip the doughnut over. Fry for 30 seconds, remove from the oil, and place on a paper-towel-lined rack sheet over a 12 by17-inch half-sheet pan. Make sure to allow the oil to heat to 350°F between batches.

Directions for Tuile Cookie Cups

1. Preheat oven to 350° and place 4 small cups (espresso-type) upside down on a work surface.

2. If adding toasted pistachios, line a 12 by 17-inch sheet pan with parchment paper and place nuts in preheated oven for 3 to 5 minutes. When cool, coarsely chop and set aside.

3. Melt butter over medium heat in small saucepan.

4. Stir in sugar, corn syrup, and vanilla extract, stirring constantly until sugar is dissolved (about 1 minute). Remove from heat. Stir in optional pistachios.

5. Line a 12 by 17-inch sheet pan with a silicone mat. Spoon 1 level tablespoon of cookie batter onto the silicone mat, allowing 2 inches between.

6. Bake for 6 to 8 minutes until the tuiles are lightly browned all over.

7. Remove from the oven and allow to cool for 2 to 3 minutes.

8. With a metal spatula (preferably an offset spatula), carefully remove each cookie and drape over one of the cups, carefully creating soft folds to form a wavy cup. When cool, carefully remove the tuile cookies. Store until ready to use.

NOTE: You can create any shape with these cookies, even rolled like a cigar and stuffed with Vanilla Whipped Cream (page 213). Let your creativity fly and have fun!

Directions for Serving Chocolate Red Robin

1. Place the doughnuts in a warm 300°F oven and heat for 6 to 10 minutes. The outside should be crispy and the inside should be oozing.

2. Place warm Red Robin doughnuts onto individual serving dishes and top with a dollop of vanilla bean ice cream.

3. Place a tuile cookie on top of the ice cream, then drizzle cookie with the World's #1 Hot Fudge Sauce (page 179).

Yield: Makes 12 Tuile cookies

Prep Time: 10 minutes

Total Time: 30 to 45 minutes

Ingredients

Tuile Cookie Cups

4 tablespoons (1/4 cup) salted butter

1/4 cup granulated sugar

1/4 cup light corn syrup

2 teaspoons vanilla extract

Optional: 1/2 cup pistachios, lightly toasted and coarsely chopped

Chef's Note

Keep tuile cookies wrapped in plastic and stored in an airtight container until ready to serve.

Marvelous Meringue Cake

My dear friends Linda and Jerry Bruckheimer turned me on to this cake, and Jerry says it's his favorite dessert of all time. He knows hit movies, and he knows hit desserts. This classic meringue cake is an award winner.

If you put this dessert in the center of your table or on your kitchen counter, you'll receive a standing ovation. Classic meringue cake is light, yet rich, yet indescribable. The layers of custard pastry cream and flavorful cake will be remembered long after the meringue is gone.

You'll love the way it looks and tastes—I guarantee it.

Chef's Note

Here's an easy method for quickly warming eggs: Put them in a bowl and cover with tepid (not hot) water for about 5 to 10 minutes. When warm, the yolk breaks easily, will mix more evenly with the whites, and attain more lofty heights when whisked. They also crack more easily and are less likely to leave bits of shell in your bowl.

Marvelous Meringue Cake ❧

Yield: Makes one 9-inch
4-layer cake

Prep Time: 35 minutes

Total Time: 60 minutes

🥄 Ingredients

Sponge Cake

4 eggs, room temperature

1 cup flour

2/3 cup granulated sugar

1 tablespoon vanilla extract

Vanilla Pastry Cream Filling

1 1/2 cups milk

7 tablespoons
granulated sugar,
divided

1 piece of lemon zest,
2 inches long by 1/2 inch tall

3 large egg yolks

1/4 cup flour

1 tablespoon vanilla extract

1 1/2 cups heavy cream

Meringue

4 egg whites,
room temperature

Freshly squeezed
lemon juice,
from 1/2 lemon

1/2 cup granulated sugar

1 1/2 teaspoons
vanilla extract

Granulated sugar for garnish

Directions for Sponge Cake

1. Preheat oven to 350°F.

2. Butter and flour a 9-inch cake or springform pan.

3. Separate the eggs into 2 bowls. Beat the yolks with the sugar until the mixture is very thick and a pale yellow. Beat in the vanilla extract. Set egg mixture aside.

4. Beat the egg whites until they are stiff but not dry. Using a rubber spatula, fold one-third of the whites gently but thoroughly into the yolk mixture. Then fold in the remaining whites.

5. Sift the flour onto the egg mixture in thirds, folding it in carefully but swiftly. Do not beat the batter; fold by cutting straight to the bottom of the bowl with the spatula to lift the batter up and over the flour.

6. Once the flour is well incorporated, scrape the batter into the prepared pan. Bake at 350°F for about 25 minutes or until a toothpick inserted in the center comes out dry and the cake is golden.

7. Let the cake cool briefly on a rack. Then remove it from the pan and let it cool completely. Using a serrated knife with a long blade, slice it horizontally into 4 even layers.

8. Immediately wrap the layers in plastic wrap until you are ready to use them. If you don't plan to use the cake the same day, then wrap and freeze cake in an airtight container or sealable plastic bag. Cake may be frozen for up to 3 months.

Directions for Vanilla Pastry Cream Filling

1. In a heavy-bottomed saucepan, combine milk, 3 tablespoons sugar, and lemon zest. Bring to a boil. Remove from heat and discard the lemon zest.

2. In a bowl, whisk the egg yolks with the remaining 4 tablespoons of sugar. Whisk in the flour one tablespoon at a time until the egg yolk mixture is smooth.

3. Gradually whisk the milk mixture into the egg yolk mixture and pour the combined mixture back into the saucepan. Cook the pastry cream over medium-low heat, stirring constantly until it thickens. Continue to cook over low heat for 3 to 4 minutes, stirring frequently. Stir in the vanilla extract.

4. Remove the saucepan from heat and let the pastry cream cool, stirring it frequently to keep a crust from forming. Cover and refrigerate for at least 2 hours. Pastry cream can be made up to 24 hours in advance.

5. When ready to assemble the cake, whip the heavy cream until very stiff. Gently fold the whipped cream into the pastry cream, combining thoroughly.

Directions for Meringue

When you are ready to assemble the cake, make the meringue topping.

1. In a medium-sized bowl, beat room temperature egg whites until they are frothy.

2. Beat in the lemon juice and gradually add the sugar. Add the vanilla extract. Beat the meringue until it is very thick and glossy.

Directions for Assembling Marvelous Meringue Cake

1. Preheat oven to 500°F. To brown the meringue, you may also use a handheld blowtorch.

2. Put the bottom layer of sponge cake on a baking sheet and spread one-third of the cream filling over it, leaving a 1/2-inch margin of cake.

3. Top with another layer of the sponge cake and another third of the cream filling. Repeat with the third layer, using the remaining third of cream filling to top the sponge cake. Add the final top layer of cake.

4. Spread the meringue thickly over the cake with a knife or spatula. Gently press the spatula down on the meringue and lift it straight up to form decorative peaks.

5. Sprinkle the cake with a little sugar, then place cake in the oven for 2 to 3 minutes to slightly brown the meringue. Watch it carefully to ensure that it doesn't burn. Remove from oven as soon as it looks good.

   If you prefer, you may also use a handheld blowtorch to brown the meringue instead of the oven. Take care not to get the flame too close to the meringue or it will burn!

Carefully slide the cake onto a serving dish and chill until ready to serve.

Marvelous Meringue Cake

❧ Little Italy Cream Cake

If you ever have the time to visit the many famous towns in Italy and marvel at the art, cuisine, and pastries, do it. Then contact me and tell me all about your trip, because I haven't been to any of those towns.

But alas, I have walked the streets of Little Italy in New York City and enjoyed the finest Italian cuisine North America has to offer. After dinner in Little Italy, a casual stroll lets you know that there may still be room to sample a fresh pastry from one of the many bakeries competing for your palate.

Years ago, I was fortunate to make the correct choice and walked into a bakery that was serving freshly baked slices of what I now call "Little Italy Cream Cake."

This cake is rich and moist, well balanced, and the frosting will have you shouting "Mama mia!"

Little Italy Cream Cake ❦

Yield: Makes one 9-inch 3-layer cake

Prep Time: 30 minutes

Total Time: 75 minutes

🥄 Ingredients

Little Italy Cream Cake

1 1/2 cups lard

8 tablespoons (1/2 cup) salted butter, room temperature

2 1/2 cups plus 3 tablespoons granulated sugar

3 large eggs, room temperature

3 cups plus 2 tablespoons cake flour

1 1/2 teaspoons salt

2 teaspoons baking soda

1 1/2 cups cultured buttermilk, room temperature

1 1/2 tablespoons vanilla extract

1 cup pecans, chopped, and very slightly toasted

1 1/2 cups sweetened flaked coconut

5 egg whites

Pecans for garnish

Directions for Little Italy Cream Cake

1. Preheat oven to 350°F.

2. Grease and flour three 9-inch round cake pans. Set aside.

3. In a large bowl, cream lard and butter until soft and combined.

4. Gradually add 2 1/2 cups sugar and beat until light and fluffy. Add eggs one at a time, beating well after each addition.

5. In a separate bowl, sift together the cake flour, salt, and baking soda.

6. Add flour mixture to batter mixture alternately with cultured buttermilk, beginning and ending the process with the flour mixture.

7. Beat until the batter is combined and smooth. Fold in vanilla extract, chopped pecans, and coconut, stirring by hand to combine. Set aside.

8. In another bowl, beat egg whites at high speed with an electric mixer until stiff peaks form, gradually adding the remaining 3 tablespoons of sugar.

9. Gently fold the egg whites into the batter until combined.

10. Ladle the batter into the 3 prepared cake pans. Shake the pans gently to level the batter.

11. Bake at 350°F for 30 to 35 minutes or until a wooden toothpick comes out moist but almost clean.

12. Let the cake layers cool for 10 minutes in the pans, then invert onto cooling racks and let cool completely.

Frost with Little Italy Buttercream Frosting (page 145).

Little Italy Buttercream Frosting

Directions for Little Italy Buttercream Frosting

1. In a large bowl, beat the butter, cream cheese, and salt at medium speed until soft and well combined.

2. Gradually add confectioners' sugar, beating until smooth. Add vanilla extract and beat slightly until combined.

3. Spread one-third of the frosting on top of the bottom cake layer up to the edges. Top with the second cake layer, making sure that the layers are leveled, and repeat for the second and third layers.

Spread remaining frosting onto the sides of the cake and garnish with lightly chopped toasted pecans.

Yield: Makes frosting for one 9-inch cake

Prep Time: 10 minutes

Total Time: 20 minutes

Ingredients

Little Italy Buttercream Frosting

1 1/2 cups (3 sticks) salted butter, softened

20 ounces cream cheese, softened

1/2 teaspoon salt

4 cups confectioners' sugar, sifted

2 tablespoons vanilla extract

1 cup chopped pecans, lightly toasted (for garnish)

Chef's Note

Sifting the confectioners' sugar will ensure your buttercream frosting is free of lumps. Don't skip this step!

Southern Sunset Cake

Southern Sunset Cake is easy to prepare and adds just a hint of lemon zest and orange in the frosting that inspires the "sunset" moniker. It is an excellent choice for a birthday celebration.

The Dedman family at the famous and historic Beaumont Inn in Harrodsburg, Kentucky, serves a cake like this with lip-smackin' results.

Before the sun sets, you must try this unique, delectable cake. Let's start preheating...

Chef's Note
Beating the eggs with the butter and sugar makes the lemon custard filling especially smooth and eliminates the small bits of cooked egg that can require straining.

Southern Sunset Cake ❧

Yield: Makes one 9-inch
4-layer cake

Prep Time: 30 minutes

Total Time: 75 minutes

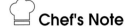 Ingredients

Southern Sunset Cake

2 cups all-purpose flour,
sifted

1/2 teaspoon cream of tartar

1 1/2 teaspoons baking powder

8 eggs, separated,
room temperature

2 cups granulated sugar

1 tablespoon vanilla extract

1/4 cup freshly squeezed
lemon juice

1 tablespoon grated
lemon zest

Lemon Custard Filling

1/2 cup freshly squeezed
lemon juice

3 tablespoons grated
lemon zest

1 1/4 cups granulated sugar

6 tablespoons salted butter

3 eggs, lightly beaten

🎩 Chef's Note

Remember: Measure the
flour first, then sift it.

Directions for Southern Sunset Cake

1. Preheat oven to 350°F.

2. Generously butter and flour two 9-inch cake pans.

3. Sift together the flour, cream of tartar, and baking powder.

4. In a large bowl, beat the egg yolks until creamy and
   increased in volume, about 5 minutes. Add sugar and
   vanilla extract, beating until well blended.

5. Fold in lemon juice and lemon zest, then gently fold the
   batter into the flour mixture, blending until well combined.

6. In a large bowl beat the room-temperature egg whites
   until it can hold stiff peaks.

7. Gently fold one-third of the beaten egg whites into the
   cake batter, then fold in remaining egg whites.

8. Spoon the batter into prepared cake pans and bake
   at 350°F for 20 to 25 minutes or until the cake begins to
   pull away from sides of the pan.

9. Remove from the oven and allow to cool for 10 minutes.
   Loosen the edges with a knife and turn out onto wire
   racks until fully cooled.

Directions for Lemon Custard Filling

1. In a medium-sized saucepan, combine the lemon juice,
   lemon zest, and sugar. Bring the mixture just to a boil.
   Reduce heat to medium-low and let simmer for 5 minutes.

2. Add butter and stir until melted. Remove from heat
   and let cool to room temperature.

3. When cool, beat eggs into the mixture until well blended.

4. Return to heat, stirring constantly for 10 to 15 minutes
   until the custard thickens and coats the back of a spoon.

5. Remove from heat and cool in the refrigerator until
   ready to use.

❧ Southern Sunset Lemon-Orange Frosting

Directions for Southern Sunset Lemon-Orange Frosting

1. In a medium-sized bowl, cream the butter until light and fluffy.

2. Add egg yolks and beat until well combined.

3. Beat in the orange zest, lemon zest, freshly squeezed lemon juice, and salt.

4. Slowly stir in the confectioners' sugar, then add the orange juice one tablespoon at a time, adding enough to make frosting creamy and spreadable. Continue beating until the frosting is creamy and light.

Directions for Cake Assembly

1. With a long-bladed serrated knife, cut each cake layer horizontally into even halves to make 4 cake layers.

2. Spread one-third of the lemon custard filling on top of the bottom cake layer, spreading to the edges.

3. Place the second cake layer on top of the lemon filling, making sure the layers line up properly.

4. Top the second layer with the second third of the lemon custard. Repeat for the third layer with the last third of the lemon filling. Add the final cake layer on top.

5. Spread the remaining lemon-orange frosting on the sides and top of the cake.

Chill cake in the refrigerator until ready to serve.

Luscious!

Yield: Makes frosting for one 10-inch cake

Prep Time: 10 minutes

Total Time: 30 minutes

Ingredients

Southern Sunset Lemon-Orange Frosting

1 cup (2 sticks) salted butter, room temperature

4 egg yolks

3 to 4 tablespoons freshly grated orange zest

2 tablespoons freshly grated lemon zest

4 tablespoons freshly squeezed lemon juice

1/2 teaspoon salt

4 cups confectioners' sugar, sifted

3 tablespoons freshly squeezed orange juice

Soufflés & Flan 🍃

Chocolate Soufflé
(page 153)

You don't need to be a master French pastry chef to create this famous French pastry. Just a few simple steps combined with the physics of heat expansion yield a fluffy dessert that brings "oohs" and "aahs" to the table. This warm, oozy experience is inspired by many tastings with Carolyn and Greg Pappas of the famous Bistro Garden of Los Angeles.

Make sure you pierce the top and load in a generous amount of fresh whipped cream or hot fudge sauce.* The spoons will be a-clankin' and you'll get a-thankin'!

Take one bite of this chocolate soufflé and you'll be saying, *"Trés magnifique!"*

Chef's Note

Tapped for time? Make your soufflés ahead of time —even the day before. Cover them and refrigerate, then bring them to room temperature when you're ready to bake. They can be refrigerated for as long as 2 to 3 days.

*The World's #1 Hot Fudge Sauce (page 179)

Chocolate Soufflé 🐇

Yield: Makes two 8-ounce (1 cup) soufflés or four 4-ounce (1/2 cup) soufflés

Prep Time: 15 to 20 minutes

Total Time: 40 minutes

🥄 Ingredients

Chocolate Soufflé

3 tablespoons unsalted butter, divided

2 tablespoons granulated sugar (to prepare ramekins)

3 ounces bittersweet chocolate chips

1/2 teaspoon vanilla extract

2 large egg yolks

2 large egg whites

2 tablespoons granulated sugar

Pinch of salt

1/4 teaspoon cream of tartar

👨‍🍳 Chef's Note

Use the bottom oven rack. Generally speaking, baking your soufflé with the rack placed on the bottom will help achieve lift. For anything light and airy that needs to rise, bake on the bottom rack.

Directions for Chocolate Soufflé

1. Preheat oven to 375°F.

2. Use 1 tablespoon of butter to grease ramekins. Coat with granulated sugar, tapping out the excess.

3. In a large bowl, microwave the chocolate and remaining butter in 30-second bursts, stirring between each burst until melted and smooth.

4. Stir vanilla extract and egg yolks one at a time into the chocolate mixture.

5. In a clean bowl, use an electric mixer to beat the egg whites, sugar, salt, and cream of tartar until stiff peaks form. Gently fold the egg white mixture into the chocolate.

6. Spoon the mixture into prepared ramekins. The soufflés can be covered in plastic wrap and refrigerated for up to 1 day.

7. Bake at 375°F for 20 minutes until puffed and set but interior is still a bit jiggly and creamy. Soufflé is done when fragrant and fully risen.

Serve with the World's #1 Hot Fudge Sauce (page 179) poured on top, or substitute with Vanilla Whipped Cream (page 213).

❧ Butterscotch Pecan Soufflé

I'll never forget the backyard at the home of my grandmother May Smith Dees in Goldsboro, North Carolina. There were three large pecan trees, and it seemed that every year there were enough pecans for squirrels and humans. I guess you could call that the balance of nature.

Fresh pecans in a butterscotch soufflé are just phenomenal. This magnificent nut imparts a buttery rich flavor that is a wonderful complement to the butterscotch.

People search far and wide for this dessert, but your search has led you here to Butterscotch Pecan Soufflé.

Thanks, Grandma, for introducing me to pecans, and then introducing me to a doctor who told me I was 25 pounds overweight.

Just kidding—I was 28 pounds overweight.

Chef's Note

Your egg whites will lift the way you want them if you start with room temperature egg whites. Whipping cold eggs is much harder work, and you won't get as much lift.

Butterscotch Pecan Soufflé 🐬

Yield: Makes six 8-ounce (1 cup) soufflés

Prep Time: 15 to 20 minutes

Total Time: 40 minutes

🥄 Ingredients

Butterscotch Pecan Soufflé

3 tablespoons salted butter

6 tablespoons (1/3 cup) granulated sugar (to prepare ramekins)

2 tablespoons all-purpose flour

4 tablespoons brown sugar, packed

1/8 teaspoon salt

1/2 cup whole milk

2 eggs, separated

1 tablespoon vanilla extract

1/2 cup toasted pecans, finely chopped

1/4 teaspoon cream of tartar

👨‍🍳 Chef's Note

You know that lovely flat top that soufflés have when you order them at restaurants? That's easily achieved with the swipe of a flat knife across the top of your soufflé right before baking.

Directions for Butterscotch Pecan Soufflé

1. Preheat oven to 325°F.

2. Butter the inside of ramekins, then dust with granulated sugar.

3. In a medium-sized saucepan on medium-low heat, combine the flour, brown sugar, and salt. Add milk.

4. Cook (stirring constantly) until the entire mixture is smooth and thick. Remove from heat.

5. In a bowl, beat the egg yolks until they are thick and yellow. Gently fold the beaten yolks into the mixture, adding the vanilla extract and toasted pecans.

6. In a separate bowl, beat the egg whites. Add cream of tartar and bring to stiff peaks.

7. Gently fold half of the beaten egg whites into the soufflé mixture, then gently fold in the remaining egg whites.

8. Pour the soufflé mixture into prepared ramekins.

9. Place in oven on bottom rack and bake for 25 to 30 minutes until puffed and golden.

10. Remove from oven. Serve immediately.

Garnish with sifted confectioners' sugar or soft dollop of Vanilla Whipped Cream (page 213).

Magnificent!

🌱 Flan "Marivi"

For a dessert as simple as flan to make it
to the All-Time Top 40 Greatest Desserts, there
has to be a touch of magic.

Let me introduce you to a flan magician named Marivi Garcia,
famous for her secret recipe she now reveals to you.

Marivi Garcia has created this flan from several
recipes handed down through generations.
Were it not for this luscious-tasting dessert,
her husband, Andy Garcia, would
never have won all the acting and
producing awards in his career.
Just ask him.

Now get ready. It's flan time!

Chef's Note
Heat the ramekins briefly in the
oven while you make the caramel.
This will make it easier to spread the caramel
and also prevent crystallization.

Flan "Marivi" 🐋

Yield: Makes 1 large 9-inch flan or six individual flans

Prep Time: 15 minutes

Total Time: 1 hour 15 minutes

 **Ingredients**

Melted Caramel

1 1/2 cups granulated sugar

Flan

1 8-ounce package cream cheese, softened

1 14-ounce can sweetened condensed milk

3/4 can (9 ounces) evaporated milk

1/2 cup water

6 eggs, slightly beaten

1 teaspoon vanilla extract

Pinch of salt

👨‍🍳 Chef's Note

Custards baked in individual ramekins cook faster, are more evenly textured, and unmold more easily.

Directions for Melted Caramel

1. Preheat oven to 350°F.

2. Cook sugar in a skillet over medium-high heat until the sugar melts and turns golden brown, 5 to 7 minutes.

If making one large flan, immediately pour the caramel carefully into a 9-inch round metal cake pan. If it stiffens before it completely covers the bottom of the pan, warm the pan in the oven, then swirl to cover the bottom.

If making individual flans. pour the caramel equally into each ramekin. There is no need to swirl the sides. Set aside.

Directions for Flan

1. Beat the cream cheese in a large bowl with a mixer at medium-high speed until soft. Add condensed milk, evaporated milk, and water. Mix until combined.

2. Add slightly beaten eggs, vanilla extract, and salt, beating until smooth. You should now have a very thick mixture.

3. Pour into the molds on top of the caramel.

4. Set molds inside a larger pan and pour into pan enough hot water (not boiling) so it comes 1 inch up the sides of the molds.

5. Bake for approximately 1 hour or until a knife inserted into the center comes out clean. Flan should be firm in the middle and slightly tremble in its center like JELL-O®.

6. Chill for at least 1 hour before serving.

Directions for Serving Flan "Marivi"

To serve, run a knife around the edge to loosen the sides of the flan, then invert onto a dessert plate.

Serve immediately, making sure to spoon plenty of the syrup over each flan.

Chef's Note

Use a cast iron skillet for melting the sugar. It works like a charm, much better than pots or saucepans.

After the caramel has hardened, butter the sides of the ramekins. This prevents the flan from sticking, making it easier to serve.

Go slow and low with the temperature. Better to slightly undercook than overcook as the flan will continue to cook once you remove it from the oven.

Before you take it out of the oven, make sure the flan really has a "slight tremble" in its center rather than a definite wobble.

Chocolate Chip Cookies
(page 167)

Chocolate Chip Cookies

The simple things in life are often the best.

This simple chocolate chip recipe is one that has beaten all competitors in cookie bake-offs® for the last 25 years. A quarter of a century of coming in at number one is worthy of inclusion in the Chocolate Chip Hall of Fame.

Sinking your teeth into these fresh chocolate chip cookies will make you want to close your eyes and purr with satisfaction. Go ahead...you deserve it.

Chef's Note
If you like your cookies soft, only a little beating of the sugar and butter will be enough.
Too much beating stiffens the cookie dough.

Chocolate Chip Cookies 🍪

Yield: Makes 3 dozen cookies

Prep Time: 20 minutes

Chill Time: 2 hours

Total Time: 3 hours

 **Ingredients**

Chocolate Chip Cookies

2 1/2 cups (5 sticks) unsalted butter, room temperature

1 1/4 cups light brown sugar

1 cup granulated sugar

2 large eggs, room temperature

2 teaspoons vanilla extract

1 1/2 cups cake flour

1 1/2 cups bread flour

1 1/4 teaspoons baking soda

1 1/2 teaspoons baking powder

1 1/2 teaspoons salt

1 pound (16 ounces) bittersweet chocolate pieces (minimum of 60 percent cacao recommended)

Pinch of sea salt

👨‍🍳 Chef's Note

Feel free to strategically place your chocolate chips. Take a few chocolate chips from the dough bowl and intentionally press them into the top of the cookies to make them look extra chocolate chippy.

Directions for Chocolate Chip Cookies

1. Preheat oven to 350°F.

2. Line a baking sheet with parchment paper or a nonstick baking mat.

3. Cream butter and sugars together for 5 minutes until very light.

4. Add eggs to the mixture one at a time, mixing well after each addition. Stir in the vanilla extract.

5. Reduce speed to low, then add the dry ingredients of cake flour, bread flour, baking soda, baking powder, and salt. Mix well.

6. Drop in the chocolate pieces and incorporate into the batter without breaking them.

7. Press plastic wrap against the dough and chill in bowl for 2 to 4 hours. When ready to bake, scoop out dough in generous portions of around 2 to 3 tablespoons in size.

8. Bake at 350°F for 18 to 20 minutes until the cookies are golden brown and soft. Ten minutes into baking, sprinkle lightly with sea salt.

9. Remove the cookies from the oven and transfer sheet tray to a wire rack for 10 minutes, then slip cookies onto another rack to finish cooling.

10. Repeat baking with any remaining dough, or freeze remaining dough for later. The cookie dough can remain frozen for up to one month.

There's nothing better than feeling healthy and satisfied at the same time. This oatmeal cookie will give you that feeling. It's flavorful and healthful, and you just can't beat that combination.

You'll notice a couple of ingredients that separate this oatmeal cookie from the pack, with a combination that qualifies it for inclusion in this special collection of the world's finest desserts.

It's a great recipe for beginners because unless you leave the oven on and take a two-week trip, you'll pull this one off.

Mix and bake your oatmeal cookies and enjoy them in record time.

Chef's Note

For a chewy cookie: Use only old-fashioned oats, not quick or instant. Coarsely grind one-fourth to one-third of the oats in a food processor or blender, then mix with the rest of the oats and proceed.

Oatmeal Cookies 🍂

Yield: Makes 2 dozen cookies

Prep Time: 10 minutes

Total Time: 20 minutes

🥄 Ingredients

Oatmeal Cookies

3/4 cup cream cheese, softened

3/4 cup granulated sugar

3/4 cup light brown sugar, packed

2 eggs

1 tablespoon vanilla extract

1 1/4 cups all-purpose flour

1 teaspoon baking soda

3/4 teaspoon ground cinnamon

1/2 teaspoon salt

2 3/4 cups rolled oats

1/2 cup flaked coconut

1/2 cup raisins

1/2 cup pecans, chopped

👨‍🍳 Chef's Note

If you have the time, place the prepared cookie dough in the refrigerator for 1 or 2 hours. Chilling the dough will keep the cookies from spreading out in the oven. Even if you need to hide the cookie dough (to prevent random and frequent taste testing), it's worth it.

Directions for Oatmeal Cookies

1. Preheat oven to 375°F.

2. In large bowl, cream together the cream cheese and sugars. Beat in the eggs and vanilla extract until light and fluffy.

3. In a separate bowl, mix the flour, baking soda, cinnamon, and salt.

4. Slowly beat the flour mixture into the cream cheese mixture.

5. Stir in the oats, coconut, raisins, and pecans until fully mixed.

6. Drop by the spoonful onto ungreased cookie sheets.

7. Bake at 375°F for 8 to 10 minutes or until the cookies just begin to brown around the edges. Remove from oven and let finish cooking outside the oven. When firm, transfer cookies to cooling rack.

8. Repeat baking with any remaining dough, or store remaining dough in the refrigerator for later use. Saved dough should be rolled into a tube on parchment paper, then placed into a sealable plastic bag.

Shortbread Cookies

These tasty cookies are always a hit with tea, coffee, and many desserts, especially White Chocolate Macadamia Nut Bread Pudding (page 183) and Butterscotch Pots de Crème (page 199).

Bake some today—you deserve it!

Directions for Shortbread Cookies

1. Preheat oven to 325°F.

2. Mix dry ingredients of flour, tea, and salt.
   Our secret: Use a wire whisk to mix the dry ingredients all together first. This will fluff it up so it blends easily with the dough.

3. In a large bowl, cream the butter and sugar until light and fluffy. Add vanilla extract.

4. Gently stir the flour mixture into the cream mixture a little at a time until well incorporated. As the dough becomes crumbly, place the dough onto a countertop or pastry board and work it together by hand until smooth.

5. Flatten the dough into a disk shape, wrap in plastic wrap, and chill for at least 1 hour or until firm.

6. Remove dough from refrigerator and pat or roll out into a 1/2-inch-thick rectangle. Cut the dough into small circles, squares, rectangles, diamonds, or use a cookie cutter to make your favorite shapes.

7. Place parchment paper on top of an ungreased baking sheet and arrange the cookies so that they are evenly spaced. Chill in the refrigerator once more for about 15 minutes. Well-chilled dough ensures the cookies won't start to melt before the starch in the cookies is set.

8. Remove dough from the refrigerator and bake at 325°F for 20 to 25 minutes until the bottom edges just start to brown. Cool on a wire rack.

Yield: Makes 2 1/2 dozen cookies

Prep Time: 15 minutes

Chill Time: 1 hour 15 minutes

Total Time: 1 hour 30 minutes

Ingredients

Shortbread Cookies

2 1/2 cups all-purpose flour

2 teaspoons ground English Breakfast tea

Pinch of salt

1 cup (2 sticks) salted butter, softened

1/2 cup brown sugar, lightly packed

1 teaspoon vanilla extract

Chef's Note

Bake shortbread in the top third of your oven. This way you won't get too much lower heat that will cause the bottom of the shortbread to overcook before the top is done.

Crowd Pleasers

White Chocolate Macadamia Nut Bread Pudding
(page 183)

World's #1 Hot Fudge Sauce

Years ago I went on a mission to find the greatest hot fudge sauce in the world. Mission accomplished!

It's obvious that a hot fudge sundae is nothing without a special secret hot fudge sauce. Well, now you're going to discover the secret.

When you ladle this hot fudge sauce over a gourmet ice cream, you will marvel at the balance of texture and enticing flavor. Personally, I have never tasted anything from a supermarket that comes close to this hot fudge sauce.

Keep the sauce in the refrigerator and pop it into the microwave for a quick emergency dessert...say around midnight.

Chef's Note

Once you make this hot fudge sauce you're going to want to hoard it, hide it in the back of the refrigerator so no one can find it, and only eat it when everyone's gone and you're alone. We fully understand.

World's #1 Hot Fudge Sauce

Yield: Makes 2 cups of sauce

Prep Time: 10 minutes

Total Time: 15 minutes

🥄 Ingredients

World's #1 Hot Fudge Sauce

3/4 cup heavy cream

3 tablespoons salted butter, cut into small pieces

1/2 cup granulated sugar

1/3 cup dark brown sugar, packed

1/4 teaspoon salt

2 heaping tablespoons unsweetened cocoa, sifted

1/2 cup chocolate chips, preferably 60 percent cacao

1 tablespoon vanilla extract

Directions for the World's #1 Hot Fudge Sauce

1. In a heavy 1-quart saucepan, warm the heavy cream and butter over medium heat. Stir until the butter melts and the cream begins to slightly bubble around the edges.

2. Add the sugars and stir for a few minutes until dissolved. Taste-test over low heat; you shouldn't taste or feel any sugar granules.

3. Reduce heat. Add salt, unsweetened cocoa, chocolate chips, and vanilla extract. Stir briskly with a small wire whisk until smooth.

Remove from heat and serve immediately.

Store in the refrigerator in a straight-sided glass jar or any container that flares out at the top. Sauce will become firm when chilled.

If reheating, place container into hot water until the sauce melts around the edges. Place in a double boiler over hot water and stir frequently, adding a bit of hot water if sauce is too thick.

White Chocolate Macadamia Nut Bread Pudding

Travel to Stanford, Kentucky, sometime. This lovely small town in the middle of the Bluegrass State has a warmth and character all its own.

On Main Street, follow the smiling crowd to the world-famous Bluebird Café, where Angela and Jess Correll have elevated their farm-to-table food philosophy to the highest level.

The unbridled creativity of chef William B. Hawkins of the Bluebird Café has inspired one of the most flavorful desserts imaginable. You'll love the rich taste of White Chocolate Macadamia Nut Bread Pudding. Each ingredient adds to a tasty team that makes the sum even more enjoyable than its individual parts.

Even if you haven't had a chance to visit the Bluebird, enjoy a generous serving of White Chocolate Macadamia Nut Bread Pudding. It'll make you feel like you've visited your old Kentucky home.

Chef's Note

Leave the crusts on, for pieces of bread crust add additional texture to bread pudding, especially on top where they crisp up.

White Chocolate Macadamia Nut Bread Pudding ◂◌

Yield: Makes one 9 by 13-inch bread pudding

Prep Time: 25 minutes

Total Time: 75 minutes

 Ingredients

White Chocolate Macadamia Nut Bread Pudding

4 eggs, beaten

1 cup brown sugar, packed

3 cups heavy cream

1 cup 2% low-fat milk

1/2 cup (1 stick) salted butter, melted and divided

2 teaspoons vanilla extract

1 1/2 teaspoons cinnamon

1 3.35-ounce jar macadamia nuts

8 ounces white chocolate, chopped

7 cups day-old brioche, croissant, or sweet Italian bread (or a mix of all 3)

🎩 Chef's Note

Securely cover the bread pudding with aluminum foil for the first 30 minutes of baking. This ensures even cooking and keeps the top from drying out.

Directions for White Chocolate Macadamia Nut Bread Pudding

1. Preheat oven to 350°F.

2. Grease a 9 by 13-inch pan. Set aside.

3. In a large bowl, whisk the eggs, brown sugar, heavy cream, milk, and 1/4 cup melted butter until well combined.

4. Add the vanilla extract, cinnamon, macadamia nuts, and white chocolate and mix well.

5. Cut the day-old bread into 1 1/2-inch cubes. Add the cubed bread and mix well.

6. Stir in the remaining 1/4 cup butter. Pour into the prepared 9 by 13-inch pan.

7. Bake at 350°F for 1 hour or until firm.

8. Let cool for 15 minutes and top with Coconut Rum Crème Anglaise (page 185).

Serve with homemade Shortbread Cookies (page 175).

Coconut Rum Crème Anglaise

Directions for Coconut Rum Crème Anglaise

1. Whisk the egg yolks until smooth and pale.

2. In a small saucepan, combine the milk, sugar, and vanilla extract. Stir frequently over medium heat. Remove from heat just before the milk begins to boil.

3. Temper the yolks by slowly adding the hot milk mixture into the egg yolks while continuously whisking.

4. Pour the mixture back into the saucepan. Continue cooking over a low heat, stirring continuously with a wooden spoon, until the mixture thickens enough to coat the back of the spoon.

5. Place the saucepan in an ice-water bath and allow the mixture to cool completely. If you cook the sauce too long or don't cool it quickly enough, the egg yolks will clump and the sauce, though delicious, will have the texture of scrambled eggs.

6. Stir in the coconut rum. Start with less and add more to taste.

Serve on the side, or drizzle on top of the bread pudding.

Yield: Makes 2 cups
Prep Time: 10 minutes
Cool Time: 30 minutes
Total Time: 40 minutes

Ingredients

Coconut Rum Crème Anglaise

4 egg yolks

1 cup milk, cold

3 tablespoons granulated sugar

1 teaspoon vanilla extract

4 tablespoons coconut rum (to taste)

⟨⊙⟩ **Date Shake**

On the road to Palm Springs, California, with the heat waves rising from the desert like translucent tongues, you can see the sign up ahead: Date Shakes.

The first time I saw the sign, I asked, "What is a date shake?" I found out and I'm glad I did, because it's time to share this phenomenal taste with you.

A date shake is basically a milkshake with pureed dates. It sounds like a simple combination, and it is. But the flavor is beyond description.

I cannot tell you how many times I've made a date shake for a friend only to have him or her say, "What's in this? It's incredible!"

I would always say, "It's an old family secret."

Use fresh dates if you can, and make sure you take out the pits. *Duh.*

Date Shake

Yield: Makes one 8-ounce shake

Prep Time: 10 minutes

Total Time: 15 minutes

Ingredients

Date Shake

4 large pitted dates, coarsely chopped

1 teaspoon vanilla extract

1/4 cup almond milk or whole milk, cold

1 1/4 cups vanilla bean ice cream

Pinch of cinnamon (optional)

Chef's Note

Garnish your date shake with homemade chocolate curls (page 189). They're extremely easy to make and add exactly the right touch.

Directions for Date Shake

1. In a blender, blend the dates, vanilla extract, and milk until smooth and very frothy.

2. Add the ice cream and pulse a few times until just blended.

3. Pour the shake into a tall glass. Garnish with a pinch of cinnamon, if desired.

Homemade chocolate curls are easier than you think...and can be used to dress up cakes, pies, shakes—just about anything!

Directions for Chocolate Curls

Have ready a large cookie baking sheet, jelly roll pan, or baking pan. Any size will do, but it should be able to fit in your freezer.

1. Melt chocolate over a double boiler until ALMOST melted, stirring constantly. Remove from heat and stir completely. Or in a microwave-safe bowl, microwave chocolate in 30-second bursts until chocolate is fully melted.

2. With a large offset frosting spatula, spread the melted chocolate out onto the back of a cookie baking sheet, spreading it out until it is in a very, VERY thin layer.

3. Put the cookie sheet into the freezer for about 3 to 5 minutes until the chocolate is almost firm to the touch, but NOT fully set. To check, press the chocolate with your fingertip: It should leave the slightest mark, but not an actual depression.

4. To create the curl: With the same offset spatula or a pastry cutter, slowly begin to scrape the chocolate at a 30- to 45-degree angle from the back of the pan. The chocolate will easily curl, especially if it's at the right temperature.

   If the chocolate is too brittle, give it a moment or two to warm up, then try again. If it gets too soft, pop it back in the freezer for a minute or two.

5. With a toothpick, transfer the curls to a cold pan or plate, and then stick them in the freezer to harden.

Store curls in the freezer in a sealable zip bag until ready to use.

Yield: Makes enough curls for 1 pie or full-layer cake

Prep Time: 15 minutes

Total Time: 20 minutes

Ingredients

Chocolate Curls

4 ounces bittersweet chocolate, in pieces or chips

Chef's Note

Because the heat of your hands can melt or mar the curls, use a toothpick as a tool to lift the delicate curls and arrange them on your cake, pie, or date shake.

For cakes: Carefully press chocolate curls onto fresh frosting. The gooey frosting acts like glue to hold the curls in place.

Bananas Foster

I remember years ago dining in New Orleans, Louisiana, and the waiter asked if anybody would like Bananas Foster.

"Did you say, 'Bananas Foster'?" I asked.

"Yes," he confirmed. "Haven't you ever had this dessert?"

"No, but you can start flaming it anytime."

He happily obliged. The pageantry of the blue flames licking the bananas and the brown sugar sweetness and butter made Bananas Foster an instant winner.

With a little practice at home and a little guidance here, you can perfect that same tableside technique.

As always, be careful around anything that flames, and keep children away from the stove. And wherever Foster is, I want to thank him.

Chef's Note
While fun to watch, the flames add nothing to the taste or texture of the final dish. Should you have any apprehension, don't flame. It will taste the same.

Bananas Foster ◄⟨◯⟩

Yield: Makes 1 serving
Prep Time: 15 minutes
Total Time: 25 minutes

⚲ Ingredients

Bananas Foster

1/4 cup (1/2 stick) salted butter

1 cup brown sugar, packed

1/2 cup heavy cream

2 tablespoons vanilla extract

1/4 cup banana liqueur

4 bananas, cut in half lengthwise, then halved

1/2 cup toasted pecans, chopped

Pinch of cinnamon, optional

1/4 cup dark rum

4 scoops vanilla ice cream

🎩 Chef's Note

Want to add some snap, crackle and pop? Sprinkle a mixture of sugar and cinnamon over the flames to create a sparkling effect.

Directions for Bananas Foster

Be prepared: Have a fire extinguisher or heavy skillet lid handy in case you need to put out the flames.

1. In a heavy skillet, melt the butter over medium-high heat. Add the brown sugar, stirring for a couple of minutes until well combined.

2. Add the heavy cream and vanilla extract, blending well. Stir in the banana liqueur.

3. Add the bananas, dropping slices into the pan. Add the chopped toasted pecans. Dust with cinnamon if desired.

4. Carefully stir in the rum. Let mixture begin to bubble, then carefully use a long lighter to ignite it.

5. Let the flame burn and go out. It should flame out naturally after about 30 seconds.

6. When the flames subside, lift the bananas from the pan and place 4 pieces over each portion of ice cream.

Generously spoon warm sauce over the top of the ice cream and serve immediately.

Extras ❧

Caramel Sauce
(page 217)

Crème Fraîche

Yield: Makes 2 cups crème fraîche

Prep Time: 5 minutes

Inactive Time: 24 hours

Total Time: 24 hours, 5 minutes

 Ingredients
Crème Fraîche

2 cups heavy whipping cream

3 tablespoons cultured buttermilk

Chef's Note

Look for pasteurized, not ultra-pasteurized heavy whipping cream. Make sure to use cultured buttermilk; otherwise, you will wait a full day to see nothing happen.

While crème fraîche does take a day to make, this thick and velvety sour cream is very easy and worth the wait. Once you taste your own homemade crème fraîche, you'll want to make it all the time.

Directions for Crème Fraîche

1. In a medium-sized bowl, combine heavy cream and cultured buttermilk. Pour into a clean glass jar or container.

2. Cover with cheesecloth, a cloth napkin, or any breathable cloth material. Let sit at room temperature (70 to 75°F) in a draft-free place for 24 hours until thickened.

3. Stir and refrigerate until ready to use. The cream will keep for about 2 weeks in the refrigerator.

Yep—it's THAT easy.

Vanilla Whipped Cream

Whipped cream with a hint of vanilla is the perfect accompaniment for your favorite desserts...and is so easy.

Yield: Makes 2 cups whipping cream

Prep Time: 10 minutes

Total Time: 15 minutes

Directions for Vanilla Whipped Cream

1. In a large bowl, beat heavy cream, sugar, and vanilla extract until stiff peaks form.

2. Cover and chill until ready to use.

Ingredients

Vanilla Whipped Cream

1 1/2 cups heavy cream

1/4 cup sugar

1 teaspoon vanilla extract

Dark Chocolate Frosting ❧

Yield: Makes frosting for one 10-inch cake

Prep Time: 10 minutes

Total Time: 15 minutes

Ingredients

Dark Chocolate Frosting

1/2 cup (1 stick) salted butter

4 ounces unsweetened chocolate (2/3 cup if using chocolate chips)

1 cup unsweetened cocoa powder

1/2 teaspoon salt

3 cups confectioners' sugar, sifted

1/2 cup evaporated milk

2 tablespoons vanilla extract

Directions for Dark Chocolate Frosting

1. In a medium-sized saucepan, slowly melt butter, chocolate, cocoa powder and salt over low heat. Stir until well combined, then remove from heat.

2. Gradually blend in confectioners' sugar, evaporated milk, and vanilla extract. Beat until smooth.

Spread generously on your favorite layer cake.

❧ Super-Creamy Chocolate Frosting

Directions for Super-Creamy Chocolate Frosting

1. Melt chocolate over hot water or using microwave, heating for 30 seconds. Stir, then heat once more for 30 more seconds. Stir until smooth.

2. In a medium-sized bowl, combine melted chocolate, unsweetened cocoa powder, salt, hot water, and confectioners' sugar. Beat on medium speed until smooth and well combined.

3. Add the egg yolks, softened butter, and vanilla extract. Continue beating until the frosting is thick.

4. Set the bowl in ice water or in the refrigerator for 10 minutes. This helps the frosting to set up.

Frost that cake!

This recipe is an excellent frosting for fudge brownies, too.

Yield: Makes frosting for one 10-inch cake

Prep Time: 15 minutes

Total Time: 20 minutes

Ingredients

Super-Creamy Chocolate Frosting

4 ounces unsweetened chocolate (2/3 cup if using chocolate chips)

1/4 cup unsweetened cocoa powder

1/2 teaspoon salt

1/2 cup hot water

3 cups confectioners' sugar, sifted

4 egg yolks

1/2 cup (1 stick) salted butter, softened

2 tablespoons vanilla extract

1 bowl ice water (to cool frosting)

Vanilla Buttercream Frosting 🌹

Yield: Makes frosting for one 10-inch cake

Prep Time: 10 minutes

Total Time: 15 minutes

🥄 Ingredients

Vanilla Buttercream Frosting

2 cups (4 sticks) salted butter, softened

1/2 teaspoon salt

4 cups confectioners' sugar, sifted

6 tablespoons milk or half & half

2 tablespoons vanilla extract

Directions for Vanilla Buttercream Frosting

1. Beat the butter and salt for 1 to 2 minutes on medium speed.

2. While beating, gradually add the confectioners' sugar, alternating with milk. Add the vanilla extract.

3. Beat until the desired consistency is reached, being careful not to overbeat. If frosting gets too thick, add a tablespoon of milk and beat until frosting reaches the desired consistency.

Frost cake generously!

Caramel Sauce

Caramel sauce is easy to make and goes especially well when paired with Butterscotch Pots de Crème (page 199).

Directions for Caramel Sauce

1. In a large, heavy-bottomed saucepan, combine the sugar and water. Heat over medium heat for about 15 minutes or until the sugar turns a deep amber color and is fragrantly nutty.

2. Add the butter and stir until it melts and is thoroughly incorporated. Be careful: It will steam and bubble vigorously!

3. Add a little of the heavy cream and stir. The caramel will begin to seize. Add a little more cream, stirring constantly. Then add the rest of the cream, stirring until well incorporated.

4. Remove the caramel from the heat and set aside.

Covered and refrigerated, the caramel will keep for up to 2 weeks.

Yield: Makes 3 to 3 1/2 cups caramel sauce

Prep Time: 5 minutes

Total Time: 15 minutes

Ingredients

Caramel Sauce

2 cups granulated sugar

1/2 cup water

3/4 cup (1 1/2 sticks) salted butter

1 cup heavy cream

Chef's Note

Before adding liquid to caramel, place a mesh strainer over the pan. Pour the liquid through the strainer. This will prevent any hot liquid from splattering on you, while allowing the copious amount of steam to escape.

Date Sauce 🌿

Yield: Makes 3 cups date sauce

Prep Time: 10 minutes

Total Time: 15 minutes

🥄 Ingredients

Date Sauce

8 ounces fresh dates, chopped

1 tablespoon vanilla extract

3/4 cup water

2 tablespoons all-purpose flour

3/4 cup sugar

1/3 cup salted butter, melted

Directions for Date Sauce

1. Puree dates, vanilla extract, and water in a blender, then pour mixture into a saucepan.

2. In a small bowl, mix together the flour and sugar. Add dry ingredients to the date mixture.

3. Add the melted butter and stir well.

4. Heat mixture and continue stirring until sauce reaches the desired consistency. To lessen the thickness, simply add a little water.

Pour the date sauce into gravy boats and ladle while still hot over a cake or your favorite dessert.

Amazingly Easy & Fast Pie Crust

Rick's spin on this fast, super-easy pie crust saves you time when you need a flaky pie crust in a hurry. Keep one box of Betty Crocker® Pie Crust Mix in your pantry and you'll always be ready!

Directions for Pie Crust

1. Prepare the Betty Crocker® Pie Crust Mix according to package directions.

2. Here's the secret: Cut 1/4 cup (1/2 stick) of butter into little pieces and combine them into the mix as you add the cold water. These tiny butter bits make all the difference.

This recipe makes 2 crusts, so save 1 for another pie.

Yield: Makes 2 flaky pie crusts

Prep Time: 5 minutes

Total Time: 10 minutes

Ingredients

Amazingly Easy & Fast Pie Crust

1 box Betty Crocker® Pie Crust Mix

1/3 cup ice cold water

1/4 cup (1/2 stick) salted butter, cold, and broken up into tiny bits

Rick's Old-Fashioned Apple Pie
(page 23)

Boston Cream Pie
(page 61)

"Something tells me you'd like another slice..."

— Chef Dees

Acknowledgments

It is a joy to acknowledge God for giving the world the sweetest of all natural ingredients: LOVE. My prayer is that you will share the goodness of these desserts and spread love to those in need.

Julie, Kevin, and Kristen Dees, thanks for saying, "mmm...GOOD!" so often.

This book came to life thanks to the encouragement and support of Kristen Chocek Dees. She is a true blessing.

A debt of gratitude to my sister Carolyn Dees Caddell for her encouragement and to her husband, Colin, with dessert experts Karen, David, and Lauren.

Special thanks go to the amazingly talented people who made this book so much fun to create. Diana DeLucia's photography and eye for detail are second to none. The editing eyes of Diane Dalbey and Nikita Colletta remind me of those of a hawk. The world-class pastry artists who baked each "Deesert" to perfection have shown me what it takes to be the best of the best. Rhy Waddington, Jamie Colboth-MacLeod, Dana Iannelli, and Leo Bushey make each dessert look like it's number one.

Maximum thanks go to Ken Lowe and pastry superstar Julia Baker Lowe for their guidance and to Wayne and Barbara Lowe, who are sweeter than any dessert in this book.

Thanks to Moose for saying, "Got anything with chocolate in it?"

My deepest thanks to the sweetest staff in Kentucky at Sweetbrier Farm.

Gracias and merci to the Choceks and Fykes for your support.

Calorie counting and certified *Desserts* auditing were performed at the highest level by Ed White and his team at Edward White & Company of Los Angeles.

Thank you, Don Krebs, for carrying my sister Patsy's beautiful wedding cakes and for your courage in carrying her through ALS.

Darden Elise Mock and Samantha Shelton have been an inspiration to all of us.

How could I love baking so much without my beautiful mom, Ann Dees, driving me in her 6-cylinder, light-blue Comet station wagon to my "Cooking Merit Badge" interview on the road to attaining the rank of Eagle Scout.

I cherish my father, Rigdon O. Dees, Jr., and his life lessons, such as "Clean up as you go."

Blessings to the dessert-loving McWhirter family: Margaret, F.T., Mark, Mac, and Ginny and Erik Hafkey.

Linda and Jerry Bruckheimer, you must be acknowledged as wonderful and talented friends who look fabulous and still love to enjoy my Peach Cobbler with ice cream.

The *All-Time Top 40 Greatest Desserts* would not exist without the dessert-loving team on the *Rick Dees Weekly Top 40 Countdown*® and millions of listeners around the world.

A shout-out to Joe Kieley, Amber, Jim Morey, and Tom Jennings who said to "add more butter." Conversion tables and measurement math were supervised by Kalfie and Dr. Jacob Van Zyl.

Mega-thanks to Jim Nehlsen and Steve Lawler who sampled my first pecan pie and asked for more. Jess and Angela Correll, thanks for rendering fresh lard at your Plainview Farm.

Thanks to Kelly Phipps, Vic Cochran, Jim Mitchell, Bob Rodman, Johnny Sparrow, and Bill Worley who shared banana splits at Guilford Dairy in Greensboro, North Carolina.

I must acknowledge all of the extremely talented performers, programmers, and executives with whom I have shared a "slice" of show business.

Finally, allow me to acknowledge you if there is a little rush when you hear the words, "Would anyone like dessert?"

Published by Dees Creations, Inc.

Visit our websites: **RickDeeserts.com**
Or **RickDees.recipes**

Library of Congress Cataloging-in-Publishing data is available.

ISBN-13: 978-0-692-49501-8
ISBN-10: 0-692-49501-0

Printed in the United States of America
First Printing, 2016

10 9 8 7 6 5 4 3 2 1